THE
EQUITY
& SOCIAL
JUSTICE
EDUCATION

50

Also by Baruti K. Kafele

The Assistant Principal 50: Critical Questions for Meaningful Leadership and Professional Growth

The Aspiring Principal 50: Critical Questions for New and Future School Leaders

Is My School a Better School Because I Lead It?

The Teacher 50: Critical Questions for Inspiring Classroom Excellence

The Principal 50: Critical Leadership Questions for Inspiring Schoolwide Excellence

Closing the Attitude Gap: How to Fire Up Your Students to Strive for Success

Motivating Black Males to Achieve in School and in Life

ASCD MEMBER BOOK

THE
EQUITY
& SOCIAL
JUSTICE
EDUCATION

50

Critical Questions for
Improving Opportunities
and Outcomes for
Black Students

BARUTI K. KAFELE

Alexandria, Virginia USA

1703 N. Beauregard St. • Alexandria, VA 22311-1714 USA
Phone: 800-933-2723 or 703-578-9600 • Fax: 703-575-5400
Website: www.ascd.org • E-mail: member@ascd.org
Author guidelines: www.ascd.org/write

Ranjit Sidhu, *CEO & Executive Director;* Penny Reinart, *Chief Impact Officer;* Genny Ostertag, *Senior Director, Acquisitions and Editing;* Julie Houtz, *Director, Book Editing;* Liz Wegner, *Editor;* Thomas Lytle, *Creative Director;* Donald Ely, *Art Director;* Melissa Johnston, *Graphic Designer;* Keith Demmons, *Senior Production Designer;* Kelly Marshall, *Production Manager;* Shajuan Martin, *E-Publishing Specialist;* Christopher Logan, *Senior Production Specialist*

PAPERBACK ISBN: 978-1-4166-3017-3   ASCD product #121060
PDF E-BOOK ISBN: 978-1-4166-3018-0; see Books in Print for other formats.
Quantity discounts are available: e-mail programteam@ascd.org or call 800-933-2723, ext. 5773, or 703-575-5773. For desk copies, go to www.ascd.org/deskcopy.

ASCD Member Book No. FY21-7 (May 2021 P). ASCD Member Books mail to Premium (P), Select (S), and Institutional Plus (I+) members on this schedule: Jan, PSI+; Feb, P; Apr, PSI+; May, P; Jul, PSI+; Aug, P; Sep, PSI+; Nov, PSI+; Dec, P. For current details on membership, see www.ascd.org/membership.

Library of Congress Cataloging-in-Publication Data
Names: Kafele, Baruti K., author.
Title: The equity and social justice education 50 : critical questions for improving opportunities and outcomes for Black students / Baruti K. Kafele.
Other titles: Equity and social justice education fifty
Description: Alexandria, VA : ASCD, [2021] | Includes bibliographical references and index.
Identifiers: LCCN 2021004463 (print) | LCCN 2021004464 (ebook) | ISBN 9781416630173 (Paperback) | ISBN 9781416630180 (PDF)
Subjects: LCSH: Educational equalization--United States. | Social justice--Study and teaching--United States. | Blacks--Education--United States. | Discrimination in education. | Critical pedagogy--United States.
Classification: LCC LC213.2 .K33 2021 (print) | LCC LC213.2 (ebook) | DDC 379.2/60973--dc23
LC record available at https://lccn.loc.gov/2021004463
LC ebook record available at https://lccn.loc.gov/2021004464

30 29 28 27 26 25 24 23 22 21   2 3 4 5 6 7 8 9 10 11 12

I know definitively that if George Floyd and Breonna Taylor were alive today, I would not have written this book at this juncture in my literary journey. Their deaths compelled me to write this book now, so it is only right and fitting that I dedicate The Equity & Social Justice Education 50 *to their memories.*

THE EQUITY & SOCIAL JUSTICE EDUCATION 50

Critical Questions for **Improving Opportunities and Outcomes for Black Students**

Introduction

Sometime between 2016 and 2017, I observed a seismic shift in the education landscape that centered around one word: *equity*. It was quite interesting for me because, prior to that time, my use of the word was solely associated with home ownership and the net worth of a home. When I started hearing various lecturers going hard on the word, I paid attention. In fact, it resonated with me on a personal level in a way that nothing else in education has in my 33 years in the field. There are so many new fads and trends that come and go in education; I pay attention to some and somewhat ignore those that, to my mind, are here today and gone tomorrow. Regarding equity, I concluded early on that it was here to stay as far as my work is concerned because I felt that, at heart, I'd always been the embodiment of an *equity practitioner* from the time I entered the education profession. I just didn't have a word to attach to it.

It is a given that we all have a story, and in most cases, it is quite inspiring and compelling. Although my story is relevant to most K–12 students, throughout my 21 years as a teacher, assistant principal, and principal, I never once shared it with my students. While I knew that my story could inspire them, at the time, I just wasn't comfortable sharing it. In fact, I prayed that it never made its way to the parents of my former classmates. And then comes this word: equity. Wow!

As the word equity emerged onto the education landscape with a vengeance, and as I was already five or six years removed from my principalship, I developed this sense of regret. I could have kicked myself for not having shared my story—where I'd come from, how I'd evolved, how I got to where I was—as so many of my students would have identified with and benefited from it. They might have viewed me through a different lens as well—one through which I would likely have appeared more relatable and relevant, a success story. In other words, the word *equity* evoked for me *individuality, identity,* and *voice.* Said differently, it evoked *student individuality, student cultural identity,* and *student voice.* Those three words—*individuality, identity,* and *voice*—and the meanings behind them, are *critical* for children in any classroom (as I will detail as we get deeper into this book).

To lend further clarity, when I refer to my story in the context of equity, I want to briefly bring you inside my academic world as a Black male who grew up in East Orange, New Jersey, with his mother and maternal grandmother during two critical decades—the '60s and the '70s. In elementary school, I was a good student. I didn't experience any academic, social, or emotional challenges. By the time I completed middle school, however, I had completely lost interest in school as a result of a variety of social and emotional challenges that arose and, consequently, led me to feel and internalize the belief that I didn't have the ability to learn and to become successful. I mean, I genuinely did not feel that I any longer had the capacity to make sense of or retain what was being taught to me in class. Throughout my high school years, I attended four high schools over a five-year period—ultimately graduating with a grade point average of 1.5! I went on to a two-year junior college, where I spent five years as a full-time student and from which I never graduated. In fact, I didn't do much more than hang out in the student center with like-minded friends (all of whom are now successful). After my stint at junior college, with nowhere near the credits needed to graduate, I enrolled in a four-year college—Kean University, here in New Jersey— and graduated summa cum laude in two years, which brings me to *equity* and *social justice.*

As I have written in various publications about the many factors that led me to get myself together and become successful, I want now to focus on two of them—discovering African American history and learning how to learn.

Discovering African American History

My first day on campus, I stumbled on an African American history book in the campus library—*To Kill a Black Man* by Louis E. Lomax—that draws parallels in the lives of Dr. Martin Luther King Jr. and Malcolm X and that completely blew my mind. I was so intrigued and inspired by what I read that I wanted to read more. Because of that book, I became a voracious reader of African American history overnight. I read *every* book about the African American experience that I could get my hands on. Why? Because reading African American history took me on a never-ending journey of self-discovery. As my eyes opened to the reality of who I was historically and culturally (my initial foray into issues of social justice), I concluded that greatness was within me and that I had no choice but to excel academically and, later on, professionally in a social justice context as a teacher and a principal. I walked into my classes with supreme confidence in my ability to excel. Through an equity lens, I was being fed what I needed to regain my confidence and become an effective classroom teacher and, eventually, school leader.

Learning How to Learn

Armed with a firm grasp of African American history, I needed a firm grasp of the mechanics of learning that spoke to *how* I learned and how my brain processed information. As I hadn't experienced academic success since elementary school, at 23, I didn't know how to achieve academic success or learn.

Instinctively, I went into each class with notebooks and literally wrote down *every* word uttered by my instructors. Absent note-taking skills, I simply wrote, word for word, both what was said and what was written on the board. I then went back to my room and studied my handwritten notes thoroughly while I read my textbooks and highlighted everything that I felt pertained to the lectures. I got to a point where I both received and anticipated receiving *A*s on exams. I maintained a 4.0 GPA throughout my tenure at Kean University, from which I graduated in 1986 as the highest-achieving African American student that year.

It wasn't until 30 years after graduating, with the onslaught of the word equity, that I definitively understood the academic transformation that I'd experienced at Kean University. Although my driving force—the study of African American history and how it was transforming the way that I viewed myself—was clear to me, the mechanics of learning was a different story entirely. As I reflected on the entirety of my K–12 years, what stood out for me was that the instruction was highly auditory. When I became a principal and, subsequently, an instructional leader, it became clear to me as I realized that many of my students were not auditory learners that I, too, was not an auditory learner. However, I had not yet figured out how I processed information as an undergraduate. When equity began to be focused on in schools, I made the connection that children in a given classroom are brilliant but it is the teacher's responsibility to discover how each student makes sense of, processes, and, ultimately, learns what is being taught. As I reflected on my transformation, I realized that I'd been successful at Kean because I was able to learn how I learn best—by *reading* what I was required to know. I learned that way then and still learn that way now—35 years after graduation. I require texts and visuals. I have to be able to *see* what I'm learning. I am a visual learner. (During my K–12 years, when auditory learning was the norm, I learned the least but was assessed based on the then-prevalent teaching norm.)

My concern is now about the elementary, middle, and high school students whom you teach and lead who may not have the wherewithal to know and to express how they learn best. Suppose that youngsters who learn visually (as I do) are being taught by a teacher whose instruction is highly auditory and are failing (as I was). Situations such as that are as prevalent as the consequences for students, both of which are contributors to the school-to-prison pipeline populated by predominantly Black and Brown youth.

As I type, I'm recalling that I turned 60 on October 22, 2020. I didn't intend to write a book (or at least not at this time), particularly not one on social justice (as I published books with ASCD in 2018, 2019, and 2020). Four of my last five books were devoted to school leadership, my primary focus of late. However, on May 25, 2020, Memorial Day, America shifted. The world shifted. We were collectively introduced to George Floyd. On that day, most of us witnessed, via cell phone video, the suffocation of Mr. Floyd by a Minneapolis, Minnesota, police officer who pressed his knee against the neck of Mr. Floyd, who was lying on the ground, for 8 minutes and 46 seconds, resulting in Mr. Floyd's death. Immediately afterward, marches, protests, demonstrations, rallies, outrage, rebellions, and riots erupted. And those activities intensified when the killing of Ms. Breonna Taylor in her Louisville, Kentucky, apartment by police officers two months prior became known. The rallying cry heard around the world was "Black Lives Matter!" I observed people of all races and nationalities with signs and raised fists expressing outrage while proclaiming that Black lives mattered.

As the days and weeks progressed, although "Black Lives Matter" was the rallying cry, because I'm an educator and look at, hear, and process practically everything from an education standpoint, what rang through my mind alongside "Black Lives Matter" was "Black Students Matter, Too." In other words, throughout the summer, the myriad challenges and obstacles associated with effectively educating Black children in America's schools weighed on me heavier than ever before in my career in the wake of the killings of Mr. Floyd and Ms. Taylor and the accompanying national outcry. I wanted to do something to change the education landscape and, for that reason, I am writing this book. I can state definitively that if George Floyd and Breonna Taylor were still alive, I wouldn't have written at this point in my career. My focus would have remained on my most recent book, *The Assistant Principal 50*, published by ASCD in May 2020.

I wrote this book so that you can examine equity and social justice education self-reflectively through an educator lens relative to the reality of students' racial, ethnic, cultural, class, religious, gender, and sexual orientation differences. Through-out the book, emphasis will be placed on equity and social justice education relative to Black children in an effort to be consistent with my motivation for writing this book—the kill-ings of George Floyd and Breonna Taylor. But also, given the reality of the so-called achievement gap in America's schools wherein Black children continue find themselves on the wrong side of this enduring gap, I want to highlight equitable strate-gies toward eliminating the Black–white gap once and for all. In 2020, Black children, in addition to finding themselves on the wrong side of the achievement gap, are perpetually on the wrong side of the disciplinary referral, suspension, expulsion, dropout, at risk, special needs referral, school-to-prison pipeline, miseducation, and any other negative gaps that one can think of. Every one of these gaps calls into question inequity in America's schools and classrooms. This must change, and to effect this change, equity must be at the heart and soul of *everything* we do. And that will require all stakeholders to walk into schools with an "equity mindset" daily.

In keeping with my previous seven ASCD books, at the core of this book are self-reflective questions designed to force you to continually look within yourself as you read. I want you to reflect on your own equity and social justice education practices as you absorb the 50 questions and commentary. My objective is to make you feel discomfort about those areas where you could be doing much more or functioning much differently and much more effectively. As I always say, I want my readers to be comfortable with being uncomfortable and uncomfortable with being comfortable.

Lastly, as always, this book is written in the second person so that you can "hear" me speaking directly to you about issues of equity and social justice relative to your students in general and your Black students in particular.

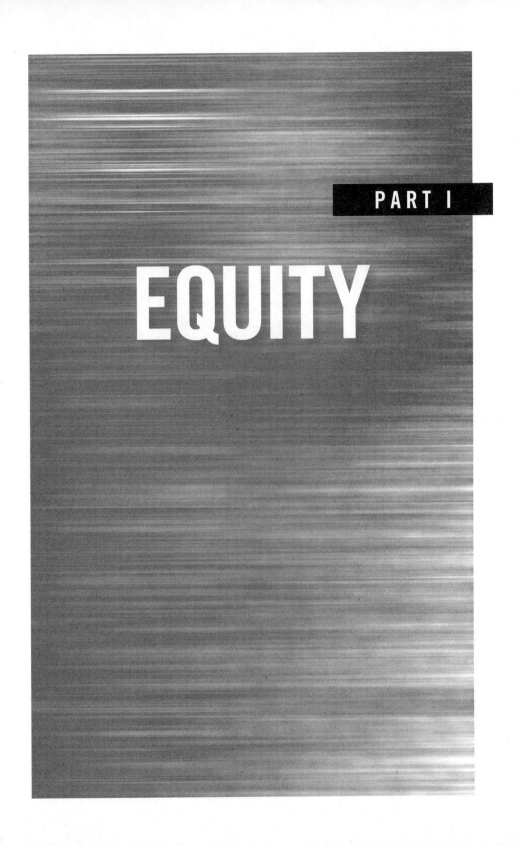

PART I

EQUITY

CHAPTER 1

Equity or Equality?

Q1 Why all the discussion around equity?

The discussion around the achievement gap has been going on for decades within and outside the education community. I can recall initially hearing about the push to close the achievement gap during my time as a first-year teacher in Brooklyn, New York, and again 10 years later during my time as a first-year principal. Shortly after I began my first tenure as a principal, the No Child Left Behind Act, which stated that all children were expected to be at proficiency levels on state standardized assessments in reading, writing, and mathematics by 2014, became law. As positive and optimistic as I typically pride myself on being, the expectation seemed overly ambitious. As the principal of my school, I said, "OK, we will get it done." In fact, my expectation was that it was going to happen well before 2014! But I couldn't help but consider the countless children across the country and the myriad socioeconomic challenges that so many of them faced from birth to the present. I felt that the goal was unattainable—and it later proved to be just that.

During my time as an educator, I concluded that expending an excessive amount of energy on variables over which I had little or no influence was an exercise in futility. I had zero control over the socioeconomic challenges that impacted my many students and their families. Although the students mattered to me dearly, I could not change their situations outside school. Where I felt I had maximum influence and control was over what they experienced in my school and classrooms. I believed that the day that I felt that I no longer had maximum influence or control was the day that I would leave the education field. How about you? Have you concluded that you have influence or control over the classroom experience of your students? Is there something about your presence in their lives that increases the probability for their success? Do you positively impact the academic, social, and emotional growth and development of your students? My desire to answer these questions affirmatively drove me to look at each student individually.

That is what equity is—looking at each student individually. Each student has their own individuality, academically, socially, and emotionally. Each student has their own cultural identity, academically, socially, and emotionally. And each student has their own voice, academically, socially, and emotionally. Each student is somebody. Each student is somebody special. Each student has his or her own set of experiences, realities, challenges, obstacles, needs, interests, goals, aspirations, and ambitions. Additionally, each student has his or her own unique way of being motivated and inspired. What sets one student on fire might not be what sets another student on fire. Most importantly, how each student learns, thinks, makes sense out of, and processes new information may be unique.

Teachers navigating the aforementioned differences is equity. Being committed to individual differences is equity. Acknowledging individual differences is equity. Addressing individual differences is equity. Intentional ongoing improvement in equitable practices is equity. Engaging in anti-racist practices is equity. And, for the purposes of this book, equity is realizing, acknowledging, and acting on the fact that the academic, social, and emotional needs of your Black students may differ greatly from those of the other students in your classroom. Ignoring racial differences and treating your students as if they were a monolithic group boils down to practicing equality, an approach to teaching that is detrimental when used as a vehicle to achieve student outcomes (as I'll address in question 7). While equality as a goal is fine, it should never be the vehicle by which a goal is achieved. *Equity* must be the vehicle by which equality is achieved. Over the years, countless students, particularly Black students, have suffered as the result of having been subjected to equality environments when an equitable learning experience was required.

Q2 Am I an equity mindset teacher?

If a classroom is going to be a truly equity-based environment, it is going to require an *equity mindset teacher*. I have thought about this deeply for the past several years. Going to conferences and trainings and reading equity-related material is good, but it isn't good enough. My contention is that one must go further than just being knowledgeable about the right thing to do. One must develop a mindset of equity. Equity must be *what* you become and *who* you are in that classroom.

I vividly recall being subjected to overt hostility while conducting a one-day equity training session with district staff. (By overt hostility, I mean that I was heckled and disrespected.) The tension in the room was palpable. Tension, discomfort, and unease are often present during equity trainings and, quite frankly, are always welcomed by me. In fact, I want the room to be filled with tension, discomfort, and unease. Discomfort can cause the person who's experiencing it to say the proverbial "ouch." It creates cognitive dissonance and, if experienced fully, forces one to change—the goal of any presenter. But in this particular case, in attendance were staff members who couldn't wrap their minds around the concept of equity, particularly along racial and ethnic lines. I was brought in because the administration felt that the disconnect between their predominantly white staff and their large Black student body was so great that grossly unacceptable levels of Black student underachievement prevailed. The tension, discomfort, and unease in the room were joined by anger, which spilled over onto my social media platforms (an occasional consequence of engaging in equity work). At the conclusion of this session, I sat in my car in the parking lot for about three hours and processed the day while feeling a deep sense of sadness for the students to whom the attendees would return the following day. I remember thinking that the district, as it realized, had a lot of work to do (which was why I was brought in). While I reflected deeply on the day in my car, I reached the following conclusion around the practice of equity:

> Equity is not solely something that you do. Equity is who you are. Equity is a reflection of the educators' humanity toward the students they serve. Equity is not a new program, model, initiative, or training. It's a way of classroom life that intentionally goes about meeting the needs of *all* learners in the classroom.

I will be the first to admit that those are indeed strong words—but I stand behind them. You can sit through an equity training and get absolutely nothing out of it if the content is in conflict with your values and beliefs. On the other hand, I would dare say that equity training ranks as one of the most significant trainings that an educator can engage in because it speaks directly to the teacher's commitment to meeting the individual needs of each and every student in the classroom. It speaks to the students' *individuality, cultural identity,* and *voice,* and goes far beyond training. It speaks to one's humanity. It speaks to who you are in that classroom. And I might add that equity work is difficult work, not so much in practice but in terms of your beliefs about who you are in your classroom and your values relative to your perceived responsibilities to your students (which we'll explore further throughout the book).

So what then is an equity mindset teacher? Throughout my travels, the term that I typically heard was *equitable practitioner.* My thinking, however, was that the teacher has to be more than just a practitioner. The teacher has to have a particular mindset, a particular attitude around equity work. Moreover, I felt that equity work, rather than be something that we shift gears into, has to be organic. It has to be something that you do naturally as an outgrowth of your compassion for your students.

As I developed my definition of an equity mindset teacher over time, I thought about the individuality, identity, and voice of students in general and Black students in particular relative to the entire teaching–learning process and concluded that an equity mindset teacher is a teacher who

> Utilizes a variety of developmentally appropriate instructional strategies that take into account the differing academic, social, and emotional needs of all learners in a student-centered, culturally responsive, and culturally relevant equity mindset classroom, where student individuality, student cultural identity, and student voice matter exponentially.

Let's break down the components of the definition in the questions that follow.

Q3 Do I utilize a variety of developmentally appropriate instructional strategies that consider the differing academic needs of my students?

I will say it until I can't say it anymore: Teaching is one of the most challenging yet rewarding occupations on the planet. It requires taking a youngster whom you may have never even seen before and nurturing a relationship with him while positioning yourself to help the youngster grow academically, intellectually, aspirationally, socially, and emotionally. The role of the teacher would be rather easy if students were the same in all regards—but that just isn't reality. Students are different along a variety of lines, such as race, ethnicity, socioeconomic status, gender, and so on. A teacher in a classroom with diverse learners must *always* consider students' differences. Students, even if they are of the same race, are different because they have their own unique experiences. All of this culminates in a diversity of academic needs in your classroom.

Imagine a classroom where, in a math lesson, the entire class is being taught a math concept using a whole-group instruction methodology for the entirety of the lesson—where everyone is receiving the same instruction at the same time and at the same pace. This is potentially disastrous for many of the students in that classroom. If I were a student in that classroom, it would be disastrous for me because of the way my brain processes math equations, which may be very different from the student sitting next to me. As my teacher, how would you account for my academic needs in this classroom? Have you considered that I may not learn at the same pace as some of my peers? Have you considered where I am developmentally in the process? Have you considered that, although I may not comprehend the concept initially, I still have the capacity and potential to excel in math in your classroom? If I am a Black student and thereby a member of a historically oppressed, underserved, and marginalized group, have you considered the uniqueness of my collective experience when you prepared the lesson? The foregoing would require that you differentiate instruction while viewing me through an equity lens—meeting me where I am developmentally.

A question that you must always ask yourself is "Do I understand how my students make sense of the information presented?" Said differently, "Do I understand how my students learn?" For me, probably the most pertinent yet basic question that you as an educator can ask yourself is "How do my students learn?" In other words, how can you best determine the most effective teaching strategies toward meeting the learning needs of all of your students, and does the reality of having Black students in your diverse classroom alter your preparation in any way? It might, when all variables are considered. An equity mindset dictates that to effectively meet the academic needs of your students, you must discover how they make sense of new information, process information, and learn.

Q4 Do I utilize a variety of developmentally appropriate instructional strategies that consider the differing social needs of my students?

Social-emotional learning (SEL) continues to be a hot topic in education. Thankfully, it doesn't seem to be one of those fads or trends that is here today and gone tomorrow. Our children cannot afford for it to disappear. As a teacher and principal of predominantly urban Black student populations (replete with all of the social-emotional challenges that accompany growing up in an urban environment) for 21 years, I recognized that social-emotional learning was at the core of our work before there was a formalized language for it. A great deal of work has gone into creating solid SEL practices in schools nationally. When it comes to learning, there's no such thing as optimally meeting the academic needs of a learner if attention isn't paid to the social-emotional needs of the learner. However, in doing social-emotional work, I have a tendency to look at the two separately. I will here examine the social needs of students through an equity lens and will in the next question examine emotional needs through the same lens.

It can never be assumed that, socially, all Black children arrive at school at the same "starting place." They have their own unique social experiences and starting places. Their experiential backgrounds dictate who they are socially. Consider a family where parents are intentional about the social development of their child, with a particular emphasis on their child's verbal communication skills. The parents are very intentional with respect to both the ability to communicate effectively and language development. This means that when they are communicating with their child, they are constantly challenging him by using unfamiliar words, with the hope he will comprehend them in the context in which they are used, and urging their child to internalize the words. Additionally, before their child is of reading age, the parents read to him daily. When he is old enough and developmentally ready to learn how to read, he begins to read on his own (which, in this case, is a requirement in this household toward further developing his vocabulary to help him become a better communicator).

Now let's consider a child whose social experience is the antithesis of that of the child just discussed. In her household, communication does not occur with the same intentionality—there's no objective attached to it; it just happens. The child is neither read to nor required to read independently when she's developmentally able to do so.

By the time both children are 3 years old and ready to enter preschool, their communication skills will probably differ vastly—because they had very different "birth to 3" experiences, *not* because one child is more intelligent than the other.

The same can be said regarding the various genres of social development and teachers' use of developmentally appropriate instructional strategies that consider the different social needs of students. Students are entering classrooms every day with differing social skills, and they have to be considered. In a true cooperative learning classroom environment, students engage with one another regularly and daily. If the students do not bring or possess the requisite social skills, there will inevitably be breakdowns in the communication process that may culminate in off-task behaviors. Therefore, it becomes incumbent on you to reexamine your focus on cooperative learning and ensure that social skill development is a part of your repertoire—which is what an equity mindset teacher will do naturally. Cooperative learning requires that attention be paid to the ways that children interact with one another. However, if there are children in the classroom whose social interaction skills are deficient, you must expend maximum attention to their social interaction skill development.

Q5 Do I utilize a variety of developmentally appropriate instructional strategies that consider the differing emotional needs of my students?

I'd planned here to share with you a detailed account of my first trauma-related experience as a middle schooler. (As I wrote it, I broke down, for the first time ever, as I recalled it and my 27-year-old witnessed his father in tears. Until that point, I'd only spoken about it and realized, after the emotional outpouring that I underwent after I'd spent quiet time writing about it, that I was for the first time fully processing it—almost 50 years later. Once I got myself together, I called my now-85-year-old mother to tell her that I was going to detail the experience in a new book and to get her thoughts. After she thought about it, she advised against it, and I took her sage advice and deleted what I'd written. Until that date, I had never shared my feeling about the experience with my mother. She was saddened to hear that I was still affected by it emotionally after so many years.) As I mentioned in the Introduction, by the time I graduated from the 8th grade, my wheels had completely fallen off, and I didn't *recover* until 10 years later, when I finally enrolled in undergraduate school. Looking back on it now (and my apologies for leaving you in suspense), my conclusion is this: For a Black boy growing up in America, life is very challenging.

I share this with you because I am using my trauma-related experience as a microcosm for so many of the children across America in general and Black children in particular who are experiencing their own trauma about which so many of their teachers are unaware. For a variety of justifiable reasons, many students have seen fit not to share their traumatic experiences with school personnel, which in many cases leaves educators to draw incorrect conclusions about their students. Black children make up about 15.2 percent of the students in U.S. public schools, while Black teachers make up 6.7 percent and white teachers make up 79.3 percent of the total teaching staff in the United States (Riser-Kositsky, 2020). This translates to thousands of Black students who potentially go through their entire K–12 experience without ever having been taught by a Black teacher. In a society that is as race conscious as the United States, and with race relations continuing to be one of the most significant issues in this country since its inception, Black children do not always have a teacher who looks like them, whom they can identify with along racial lines, and whom they can talk to about a plethora of emotional issues that a Black teacher would likely understand. In other words, let's say that there is a student who is acting out or exhibiting undesirable classroom behaviors, and the conclusion is that the student is just, for example, recalcitrant. If the teacher of said student went beyond the surface and the student opened up, it might be discovered that the student, far from being recalcitrant, is experiencing a great deal of trauma and the only way that he knows how to deal with it or even to release it is through the behaviors observed by the teacher. When you translate this to instruction, it becomes that much more challenging and complicated. The teacher is trying to teach, but the behaviors being exhibited make it almost impossible. If the teacher happens to be Black and the teacher and student have forged a relationship and rapport with one another and identify with one another along racial/cultural lines, there is a higher probability that the student will open up to the teacher. Because the student can identify with the teacher along racial/cultural lines, there's a higher probability that the student will be comfortable confiding in the teacher while feeling confident that the teacher will be able to relate to the issue. The non-Black teacher who has been intentional about forging a relationship with the student from the outset (making him feel comfortable enough to disclose the trauma that he is experiencing) is in a position to also be a resource for the student while putting herself in a better position to meet his emotional needs. It's all in the intentionality of the relationship, and it is definitely possible when this intentionality exists.

Q6 Do I provide my students with a truly student-centered learning environment?

Is your classroom all about each of your students? Do each of your students feel that your classroom is all about them? Is the individuality of each student evident? Is the cultural identity of each student evident? Is the voice of each student evident? Do each of your students have equitable opportunities to learn? Do you provide your students with a true student-centered learning environment? Do your Black students feel that they are valued in your classroom? Do your Black students feel that they have equitable opportunities for success? Do your Black students feel that your classroom is preparing them sufficiently for their next level? It is common for educators to engage in a discussion about the differences between a teacher-directed learning environment versus a student-centered learning environment, in which students are afforded the opportunity to engage in and participate in their own learning. The learning is all about the students, and they are actively engaged in the learning process. On the other hand, in a teacher-directed learning environment, instruction and learning are typically all about the teacher. The students are passive participants. The goal is that students learn not by engaging and participating in their own learning but by passively listening to and absorbing the information being shared by the teacher. A true student-centered learning environment is all about each individual student, and evidence abounds throughout the classroom that this is actually the case.

Often when we think about learning environments that are student-centered, we think about those classrooms where cooperative learning is the norm and students have daily opportunities to engage in and participate in their own learning in cooperative group settings, where they get to engage with one another on a variety of different topics and issues. I can recall numerous times in both undergraduate and graduate school when several of my professors engaged us in cooperative lessons where my peers and I, in a group, were assigned a particular problem to solve collaboratively. I recall the personal anxiety that set in every time we were instructed to "turn to your neighbors." I wanted no part of this. Despite being a teacher, principal, and public speaker, I continue to be shy and an introvert. It's who I am. I want no part of collaborative settings. As a public speaker, the anxiety intensifies for me—but not from the speaking part. I am in my comfort zone when speaking to an audience, regardless of its size. (Throughout the year, I frequently deliver keynote addresses to large audiences.) Whenever I do not have an immediate flight out, I attend follow-up breakout sessions with the conferees. Conference attendees know who the keynote speaker is, so when you walk into a breakout session room, everyone knows you are there. My intention for attending a breakout session is to learn something new because, although I was invited to deliver a keynote address, that doesn't make me the smartest person in the room. I want to grow professionally after my keynote. The problem arises when the presenter asks us to break into groups and to collaborate on solving a problem or speaking to an issue. At that juncture, I say to my peers at the table with me, "You all got this," because I want no part of it. Although I delivered a keynote to hundreds or thousands, in that group of 5 to 10 people at a table, the introvert in me comes out like clockwork. But while I can turn away and not participate and suffer zero consequences, the students in your classroom—the younger versions of Principal Kafele—aren't at liberty to utter the words "You all got this" and turn away without suffering multiple consequences.

With that said, let's revisit student-centeredness. In all schools, there are shy, introverted students as well as students who are contending with a multiplicity of challenges outside school and, justifiably, don't want to be social in class. What do you do when these students enter your classroom? How do you accommodate them? Are you aware of those students? Are you clear as to why those students have no desire to participate? Looked at differently, what if your school only has a small population of Black students and, in any given classroom, there is only one Black student on your roster and she happens to be introverted. Have you created a learning environment where this student feels comfortable, at home, and accepted by the majority of the students? My point here is that, in a true student-centered learning environment, this student's disposition is taken into account. Perhaps, like myself, she would rather learn in isolation. I say to teachers regularly, hold the youngster accountable for developing the requisite social skills in order to be able to function socially in the world beyond school, but don't necessarily measure their intellect on how they function in a cooperative setting. Treat them as two separate yet interrelated entities, but never lose sight of the fact that the classroom is all about individual students and allowing students to excel within their learning capacity of strength. Again, using myself as an example, to this day, I have difficulty learning auditorily and in cooperative settings. This is who I've been for my entire life. I am highly visual, and I want to be alone when I learn. If your classroom is a true student-centered learning environment, you will have a laser focus on ensuring that all of the students have equitable opportunities to learn based on who they are.

Q7 Is there a place for "equality mindset teaching" in my classroom?

On the surface, equality is not a bad thing at all. After all, as an African American, I was born into the struggle for equality. I was born in 1960 and grew up in the '60s and '70s in the midst of the civil rights movement—a movement for justice and equality that, although it looks different now, continues to exist in the new millennium because many of its objectives remain unmet. So I could never dispute the importance of the word equality because the quest for it for Black and Brown people, particularly, is ongoing.

In the classroom, however, equality must be looked at differently. As I referenced in my explanation of equity, equity is a vehicle to equality, but equity in and of itself can never be the endgame. In other words, you wouldn't attain the goal of being an equitable practitioner in an equitable learning environment and think that your goal had been met. You are simply on track to reach the goal. Said differently, equity becomes the vehicle to equality, but equality can never be the strategy. Equality is the goal. Equity is the strategy. Equality mindset teaching has a place in a classroom when the goal of the teacher is equality via making equitable teaching practices the norm of the pedagogy in the classroom. Children are in all different places and spaces academically, socially, and emotionally in the classroom, and an equality approach toward meeting their academic, social, and emotional needs will pretty much guarantee that an abundance of children in that classroom will spend an entire year with an outcome of unmet needs. Why? Because they were taught as though they were all the same academically, socially, and emotionally.

To delve a little deeper, on numerous occasions throughout my work as a consultant over the years, I have met "equality mindset teachers" all over America. I find it rather fascinating that they typically emerge during the equity conversation. They are so entrenched in equality mindset thinking that they typically challenge me passionately right on the spot. And to paint an accurate picture, I've always been told by younger white female teachers of Black or Latinx students something like this:

Principal Kafele, why do we have to have this discussion about race? When I am in my classroom, I do not see race. I don't see the Black students, the white students, the Latinx students. I see my students. I don't look at them the way that the world looks at them. I do not discriminate against any of them, either. I treat them all the same. What I give one, I give the other. My students are my babies, and I love them all equally and unconditionally.

Additionally, there is typically an "amen corner" in the room, which is all the fuel the teacher needs to continue to express herself about being an equality mindset teacher. I stand there patiently listening to their words every time I have this experience and respond after they've shared all of their thoughts. In all actuality, I could spend an entire session responding to those teachers' words and am well aware that there are countless others in our profession who hold the same sentiments. Therefore, the next chapter will comprise my detailed reaction and response to and solutions for any teachers out there who continue to bring an equality mindset to the classroom as the vehicle to student success, or anyone who's looking to expand their understanding and implementation of equitable practices in their classroom.

CHAPTER 2

Equity and the Individuality of Learners

Q8 Does my presence positively alter the trajectory of each of my students?

In my book *The Teacher 50* (2016), the first question reads, "Are my students at an advantage *because* I am their teacher?" In workshops, my audiences and I can spend *hours* on this question because there is just so much to dissect. America boasts more than 50.8 million school-age children, more than 3.2 million K–12 teachers, and more than 90,000 K–12 schools (Riser-Kositsky, 2020). What that means is that, although you and your students could have wound up any-where in the country, you both ended up in your state, your city or town, your district, your school, and your classroom. So the deeper question becomes, "If another teacher came into my space, would the probability of the success of each student increase? Do you matter for each student in your classroom? Does your presence positively alter the trajectory of each stu-dent in your classroom? What is the probability for success for Black students in your class? In a diverse classroom, does your presence positively alter the trajectory for each of your Black students? In your eyes, are your Black students at an advantage *because* you are their teacher?"

If you are an equality mindset teacher, it is very likely that another teacher—a teacher with an equity mindset—could come into your space and increase the probability for the success of individual students because the students wouldn't be lumped together and treated as though they were all the same. A teacher who views students through an equality lens prob-ably *doesn't* matter to each individual student because, in the name of equality, there will be many whose academic, social, and emotion needs are not met. I strongly contend that the only place for equality as it relates to strategies in a classroom is a museum; it is a relic from the past that has no place in a 21st century classroom. As the teacher, throughout the self-reflective, self-assessment process, you should ask yourself, "Do I matter to all of my learners?" "Do all of my learners benefit from my presence?" "Are my students at an advantage *because* I am their teacher?" "Does my presence positively alter the trajectory of each of my students?"

Q9 What is the *evidence* that my presence positively alters the trajectory of each of my students?

The addition of the word *evidence* changes the entire meaning of the question. It's easy to make proclamations, declarations, and assertions. Although we all, to varying degrees, make them, we must at some point back them up with concrete evidence. For example, while someone may *feel* that they do what they do effectively, what is the evidence that they are indeed effective? The title alone of my book *Is My School a Better School Because I Lead It?* (2019) forces readers to look deeply within themselves. It pushes school leaders to take an honest and earnest look at their practice as school leaders while assessing whether or not they really matter. The reason that I wrote the book and titled it thusly was because I asked myself that question every day throughout my career as a principal. In doing so, I was looking for evidence daily. It's easy to answer the question affirmatively, but what I sought to do was to remove my ego from my answer and let the evidence do all of the talking. And trust me, on many days when I asked myself that question, my answer was an emphatic no. Why? Because in being brutally honest with myself, on a given day, the evidence that the school was a better school because I was there just wasn't there—and a lack of equity, toward either staff or students, was typically the reason why. Your evidence matters.

What is the evidence that your presence positively alters the trajectory of each of your students? What is the evidence that each student is afforded the benefit of an equitable learning experience in your classroom every day? What is the evidence that your students are in a classroom where the probability for their success is high because you are their teacher? What is the evidence that all of your students matter? What is the evidence that each of your Black students is at an advantage because you are their teacher? What is the evidence that your Black students feel welcome in your classroom? What is the evidence that your Black students feel that they belong in your classroom? What is the evidence that your Black students are on a trajectory of success as a result of being in your class-room? These are questions that I strongly recommend you consider regularly in your ongoing pursuit of a truly equitable experience for all of your learners.

Q10 How do I make the distinction between equity as the *vehicle* and equity as the *goal* for each of my students?

During my presentations on equity, I use two go-to graphics. The first graphic depicts three individuals of differing heights who are each attempting to reach one of three apples hanging from a horizontally level branch of an apple tree. All three individuals are given crates of equal height to stand on to enable them to reach the apple, but only the tall individual can reach the apple while standing on the crate. In this scenario, the tall individual is the only one able to eat, which is key.

In the other graphic, the tall individual is given only one crate and the shorter and shortest individuals are given two and three crates, respectively, to stand on, enabling them all to reach the apple. In this scenario, all three individuals can reach their respective apples because they were given the assistance they needed to do so. What's key here is that equity is the vehicle to equality, not the goal. As I stated previously, equity can *never* be the goal. Equality in terms of opportunity and access are the goals, but the vehicle to get there is equity.

How do you go about making the distinction between equity as the vehicle and equity as the goal in your classroom? How do you ensure that equity is the process that you utilize to meet the academic, social, and emotional needs of your learners in a diverse student learning environment? How do you go about maintaining a mindset that all of your learners have the capacity to achieve excellence but may require different pathways to get there? In a world where Black children have historically been on the wrong side of the achievement gap, how do you ensure that *equitable* practices that enable your Black students to have *equal* access to the apple are being executed in your classroom? As the teacher, it becomes incumbent on you to ensure that equity is never allowed to become the goal and always keep in mind that it is the vehicle to attaining the goal. Teachers who bring an equality mindset to their classrooms and who, therefore, do not see the diversity in their learners are doing them a disservice, because equality becomes the vehicle by default. Student suffering in this environment is pretty much a given.

Q11 How do I ensure that no student is invisible in my classroom?

It took having a heart attack to make me fully grasp what it means to be invisible in a classroom. In an instant, I learned in a very real way what it meant to be present without having a presence. On May 1, 2015, I suffered a heart attack while delivering a keynote address at the University of Miami. Because my main artery was 100 percent clogged and I'd suffered an attack referred to as "the widow-maker," I was an emotional wreck. The following morning, I learned that I also had Type 2 diabetes. I was discharged from the hospital on May 4 and, against my doctors' wishes, returned to the speaking circuit on May 13. I knew that I had a way to go physically; I could feel it. Emotionally, however, I was ready to resume working. I felt I was ready to get back in front of audiences and do what I love. But an experience I had while traveling let me know that I wasn't quite as ready emotionally to get back to work as I'd thought. As I walked through the crowded airports in Houston, Chicago, Newark, Charlotte, and Atlanta, I felt a sense of *invisibility* that I had never experienced before. I felt like the invisible man. I felt like a ghost. I felt like no one could see me. I felt like I was there but completely transparent. I felt like I had no presence in the airport. I felt that people, as opposed to seeing *me*, saw *through* me. I was present but felt I had no presence. This feeling of invisibility lasted for several months. While I was fine when I was in front of audiences, I felt as if I wasn't there when I was in crowded airports.

Because I look at practically everything in life through the lens of an educator, this experience compelled me to think about the many Black children in classrooms across America. It made me think of myself in my high school classrooms when I felt, as I did after my heart attack, invisible. There are invisible Black children languishing in classrooms all over America. They are physically present but academically invisible. They are looked at but unseen. They speak but are unheard. These are the children who can potentially fall through the cracks. Many develop behavioral problems because they are invisible academically. When I entered my fourth and final high school (where I was enrolled by my mother in a last-ditch effort to save her only son), the environment was completely unfamiliar, and I found it intellectually daunting. I was one of only five Black students in a predominantly white school of more than 2,000 students with a predominantly white staff. I was never in a classroom with another Black student. My teachers never called on me in class. Because I was permitted to sit in the back of all of my classes (while praying that I wouldn't be called on to answer a question), I now painfully admit that I felt intellectually inferior to my white peers. I felt inadequate. I had completely bought into the false narrative that to be smart is to act white. I hadn't yet come to know my history, and it certainly was never mentioned in this school beyond superficial discussions on slavery. Not one teacher in the building challenged me to believe that I had more within me. I remained completely invisible and uncomfortable for the three years that I spent in that school every day until 4:00 p.m., when it was time for basketball practice, where I shined. (After all, it was expected that a tall, Black young man would shine athletically.) When I think of the gross disproportionality of Black students in advanced placement (AP) classes, in addition to the systemic racism that precludes their entry, I often wonder what percentage of Black teenagers may be avoiding these classes for reasons similar to those that led me to sit in the back of classrooms in the predominantly white high school I attended.

Being an equitable practitioner will require that you avoid student invisibility in your classroom. Being an equitable practitioner will require that you meet your students where they are toward making them feel that they are an inherent part of your classroom and fully realize that they are somebody special. Being an equitable practitioner will require that you be intentional about the reality of student individuality and distinctiveness and meet all students where they are. Being an equitable practitioner will require that you see each student as an individual while avoiding at all costs seeing them through one singular lens and attempting to treat them all the same in the name of equality. As an equitable practitioner, you must welcome your students' differences while helping them feel that they are an integral part of your classroom family.

Q12 Do my practices prevent racial identity obscurity in my classroom?

In Question 7, I indicated that this chapter is essentially the response to the equality mindset teacher who sees all the children through the same lens and doesn't see racial differences. To ignore, deny, or suppress a student's racial identity, whether unintentionally or intentionally, is an inherently racist practice.

It would fall under the category of implicit or explicit bias, predicated on the intent. It is equivalent to a student saying to the teacher, "If you don't see my racial identity, you don't see me. If you don't see me, you can't effectively teach me. And if you can't effectively teach me, why am I in this classroom?"

One's racial identity plays a significant role in one's overall personal identity. For example, I am very clear about the fact that I am not simply a man, but a Black man. Being a Black man is a part of my overall personal identity, but it doesn't stop there. I am reminded continually that it is also a part of my professional identity. Being a Black man (as opposed to just a man) evokes a broader personal and professional identity context. In other words, there are connotations and experiences associated with being a Black man that may not necessarily be transferrable to men of other races—historically, culturally, emotionally, psychologically, educationally, professionally, experientially, and from a health standpoint. For example, as a Black man, one of the most uncomfortable aspects of my life is driving while a police cruiser is traveling behind me. Theoretically, this should not be an uncomfortable moment if I am driving within the speed limit but, unfortunately, it is. It is downright nerve-racking for me and countless other Black men because, in today's landscape, we don't know how a traffic stop will culminate. We all know that countless times throughout American history, traffic stops have been fatal for Black drivers in general and Black male drivers in particular. It's a part of the reality of Black men. But at the end of the day, I am proud to be a Black man. If I came back into this world again, I'd want to come back as a Black man. Why? Because it is a large part of my overall personal identity, and I am proud of who and what I am.

Now what does the aforementioned have to do with student racial identity in your classroom? I'm glad you asked. Everything! The equity discussion is a very interesting one because of its origins. For the equity conversation to make complete sense, you have to go all the way back to the achievement gap conversation. Yes, we ultimately looked at a variety of subgroups and determined that there are a variety of gaps in achievement, but the gap that has always gained the widest attention—decades before No Child Left Behind—was the Black–white achievement gap. Countless programs, school reform models, trends, and fads arose over the decades to close the Black–white achievement gap, but in 2020, this gap was still the main topic of conversation in education nationally. As a part of the continuum of strategies and solutions to close the Black–white achievement gap, the word equity surfaced in the new millennium, and it became the latest focus for closing this achievement gap. Personally, I love it. It just makes sense. At the classroom level, it translates to meeting students where they are while never losing sight of who and what they are. As it relates to Black students specifically, equity translates to a commitment to anti-racist classroom practices.

I am saying all of this to say that, in an equity mindset classroom, the racial identities of your students absolutely matter. Their racial identities can never become obscure or invisible or be suppressed. Their racial identities play a large role in who they are, and as educators, we can never pretend that their racial identities do not exist. They *do* exist and are worthy of distinction, recognition, acknowledgment, accentuation, and celebration (as I'll show in Chapters 3 and 4). There are definite consequences, on multiple levels, for children when their racial identities are suppressed. For example, in an environment of racial identity obscurity where the teacher doesn't see the race of the students, the teacher has created for the students an artificial, utopian world that doesn't exist beyond the school walls. Once the students get outside, they are reentering a world that will definitely see their racial differences. The problem is that the children are in a classroom for almost 200 days out of the year where the teacher has created a false narrative and, therefore, has not prepared the students for the world beyond the classroom. The teacher must strive to write a narrative where differences are highlighted, recognized, acknowledged, accentuated, and celebrated.

Q13 In what ways do I help my students find their "voice" in my classroom?

You'll notice that I put the word *voice* in quotation marks because I am referring not to what you hear out of a student's mouth per se but instead to the student's ability to find one's self. In other words, I'm talking about students learning in an environment where they are learning content and learning *about* themselves on the path to *finding* themselves. They are discovering who they are. They are discovering their own capacities. They are discovering their own potential. They are discovering their own worth and value. They are *finding their voices.*

Many young Black males grow up with hoop dreams (i.e., dreams of playing professional basketball). This is what they see daily. This is where they see other Black men achieving fame, fortune, status, prestige, and worldwide recognition, and many of them grow up wishing to attain those things while operating under the false narrative that "that is my only ticket out." The problem arises when the realization that one isn't good enough to play sports professionally kicks in. If all of your eggs were placed in the sports basket, you may not be aware of the plethora of other options available and accessible to you. I was that young man. Until I was around 18, I just *knew* that I would become a professional basketball player. Once the reality that it wasn't an option set in, I asked myself, "What will I do?" It gradually became clear to me that I wanted nothing more than to become a teacher, and I became one at the age of 28. I found my voice and have been walking in it for the past 33 years.

What about your students and their own self-discovery, regardless of how young they may be? Are they on a pathway toward finding their voices in your classroom? Is having students find their voices a priority in your classroom? Do you see your students for who they are now as well as for what they will become as a result of having you as their teacher? The ongoing conversation, therefore, regarding the correlation between classroom performance and who and what your students will become is unavoidable when it comes to your students finding their voices.

Q14 What measures do I take toward allowing my students to feel comfortable in their own skin?

By virtue of the fact that you have children in your classroom, there is an excellent chance that a percentage of your students do not feel good about being themselves. They are students who are not comfortable in their own skin. This is one of the unfortunate realities of our profession because it is one of the unfortunate realities for countless children across America. When children enter your classroom not feeling good about themselves, the reasons why are potentially both painful and, as may be revealed through careful probing, investigation, and analysis, understandable.

Although the cliché "comfortable in your own skin" translates to how one feels about one's self, I want to take the liberty to expound on a painful literal example of not feeling comfortable in one's own skin. I have had numerous opportunities to converse with strong, darker-complexioned Black women educators who I met in my capacity as a consultant, and I learned of some of the experiences that too many of them had to endure among their Black peers when they were in grade school. A careful analysis of American history with an emphasis on the Black experience will reveal one of the numerous disturbing aspects of American history relative to the Black experience where darker-complexioned Black men and women had historically been racially caricatured in print media, broadcast media, film, and theater for many decades in deeply disturbing racist depictions that included racially demeaning and insensitive minstrel shows where white performers performed in blackface. This reality had widespread adverse implications for the Black community, and the children were not spared. Black children were exposed to these same racist depictions of darker-complexioned Black men and women throughout the generations but were afforded no historical context for the existence of these depictions. Through the generations, the onslaught of these depictions resulted into what is known as self-hatred for some, and consequently, many darker-complexioned Black children in general and Black girls in particular felt the weight of this racist past and were ridiculed, harassed, teased, and so on by some of their

Black peers in school about their skin complexion and African features and characteristics. In other words, through systemic racism, Black people were *taught* to hate themselves for more than a century. A mental, psychological, and emotional crime that mentally, psychologically, and emotionally damaged so many Black children about who and what they are racially, culturally, and historically for generations was committed. As a child who grew up in the '60s and '70s, I cannot tell you the number of times that I witnessed my peers either arguing or "playing the dozens" wherein, to add sting to an insult, they would preface the insult with the word *Black* (such as "You Black [so-and-so]"). Thirty years later as a classroom teacher, I saw the same behaviors exhibited by my students. Nothing had changed in 30 years! This is learned behavior that is rooted in a racist past that has sustained itself through time and will be around as long as textbooks and curricula continue to distort, marginalize, trivialize, or omit the history of Black people in America. Again, anti-racist practices are an inextricable component of the equity conversation.

With the normal challenges of life, this was an added burden for Black people to have to endure and ultimately overcome toward feeling completely secure, empowered, and comfortable in our own skin. This was the experience that several of the darker-complexioned Black women educators who I referenced had to endure in childhood. I have to share with you that writing this pains me to no end.

As a teacher and one who's conversant in African American history, I was in a position to head this off before it even manifested in an assortment of ways using history as my reference in my efforts to encourage my darker-complexioned Black students to feel pride in their dark skin to the extent of walking around with their chests out, shoulders back, and heads held high. But that was because I know history. The teacher who doesn't know history is at a disadvantage in this regard. Over the years, as I have engaged in this particular conversation with successful darker-complexioned Black women (and men) educators, just the mention of this topic can evoke childhood memories of pain. The good thing is that the world is steadily evolving, and pride in overall Blackness has evolved exponentially to the extent that this experience isn't as much of an issue as it was in the past.

Are your students comfortable in their own skin? Do they feel good about themselves? Are they pleased with who and what they see in their mirrors? Are you able to detect when students do not feel good about themselves? Is identifying low self-esteem or pain toward self a part of your teaching repertoire? What measures do you take toward helping your students to feel comfortable in their own skin? I cannot overstate the significance of you positioning yourself to make these observations. There are children all over the country who are hurting, who are coping with very difficult challenges in their lives that have implications for how they feel about themselves, including the volumes of children who have either contemplated or committed suicide. They did not have appreciation for how special they truly were, for the gifts they were born with, for the gifts that they were to the world, or for the potential they had to achieve whatever they wished in life. In an equity mindset classroom with an equity mindset teacher, there is a higher probability that these children will receive the attention that is required for them to get back on track. Their individuality will not go unnoticed in this environment. That they, too, are somebody special will be fully acknowledged by their teacher.

CHAPTER 3

Equity and Being a Culturally Responsive Practitioner

A Google search of culturally responsive teaching practices and cultural responsiveness in the classroom will yield an endless yet invaluable stream of results in the form of definitions, blog posts, books, articles, videos, and lectures. Although reading through too many of the results may leave you feeling as confused as you were before your search, I nevertheless urge you to engage in the exploration of what culturally responsive teaching is and is not. Toward that end, I'd suggest reading one or all of the following five go-to books on culturally responsive practices that I've read over the years:

» *Why Are All the Black Kids Sitting Together in the Cafeteria? And Other Conversations About Race* by Beverly Daniel Tatum

» *Other People's Children: Cultural Conflict in the Classroom* by Lisa Delpit

» *Culturally Responsive Teaching: Theory, Research, and Practice* by Geneva Gay

» *Black Children: Their Roots, Culture, and Learning Styles* by Janice E. Hale

» *The Dreamkeepers: Successful Teachers of African American Children* by Gloria Ladson-Billings

I consider the five Black women authors of these books pioneers and gurus in culturally responsive practices whose books should be read by all.

As I continued to read, study, research, and, ultimately, implement culturally responsive practices as a 5th grade teacher in an urban school district in New Jersey where the student body was approximately 98 percent Black and experiencing great success, I essentially though inadvertently developed the following definition (which I have since formalized) of a culturally responsive teacher:

> A culturally responsive practitioner is a teacher who continually considers what the students *see, hear, feel,* and *experience* as individuals in a learning environment that constantly affirms who they are, what they are, and what they can become as a result of their presence in their classroom and in the space of their teacher.

I refer to what students see, hear, feel, and experience as the Four Intentionalities of the Classroom—in other words, the teacher's *purposefulness* regarding what students see, hear, feel, and experience.

Q15 Toward creating a culturally responsive learning environment, how intentional am I about what my students see?

What your students see matters. Let me repeat that: What your students see matters. There was a very brief time in my early days as a teacher where my classroom was pretty much a random learning environment. What I mean by that is that, while I made the classroom aesthetically pleasing, there was no rhyme or reason as to why it looked the way that it did. Thankfully, that didn't last very long. It soon dawned on me as a young, inexperienced teacher that whatever my students could see needed an objective attached to it—a learning objective, a self-esteem objective, or a self-image objective. I wanted whatever my students saw to be an extension of my objectives for them as their teacher. Toward creating a culturally responsive learning environment, I referred to this aspect of the environment as *the intentionality of what my students could see*. Because my students were Black and growing up in an urban environment, I was highly intentional about everything that they saw in my classroom relative to their academic growth and development or building their self-esteem. Let's examine some of the items that were in my classroom.

Student Action Photos

Toward creating a culturally responsive classroom, I needed the students to feel that the classroom was truly their own and figured that there was no better way of doing that than filling a wall with action photos of my students at work. This gave them a sense of ownership and of belonging. Do you hang student photos on your classroom walls?

Student Awards

Using a little creativity, I found that I could create an award for almost anything. Many students only saw their names associated with negativity (such as detention), and I had to change that. I needed them to see their names in lights. That meant that I had to differentiate and identify their unique strengths so that I could acknowledge and celebrate them. Subject Area Students of the Week certificates were displayed on the wall. If, for example, a student excelled in just one subject area, I zeroed in on it so that I could recognize him with a certificate displayed on the wall and use that as my opening to encourage and develop the student in other subject areas for the following week. This also gave students a sense of ownership and of belonging and served as a vehicle to build self-esteem. How are you using awards in your classroom?

Student Goals

I devoted an entire wall solely to student goals. My logic for student goal setting was that, without a target for which to aim, students wouldn't strive for excellence. The goal was the target. At the start of each marking period, each student was required to set and write a grade-letter goal for each subject area taught in my classroom and to devise a strategy for achieving it. The students' goal sheets or goal cards were then posted on a wall that was labeled "Student Goals." Not surprisingly, the number of students who achieved honor roll increased exponentially—because earning high grades, rather than being a hope or a wish, was now a concrete goal that students strove to attain. This gave students a sense of belonging in a culturally responsive learning environment, not to mention what it did for their self-esteem. In what ways are you using a student goal-setting strategy in your classroom?

Student Work Samples

As our classroom family evolved and became increasingly culturally responsive, children felt good about having their work displayed. All students have strengths, and it is on us, the teachers, to identify them. I proudly displayed student work that showcased their strengths on a wall in my classroom— and on a wall in the hallway outside my classroom. Needless to say, the students felt a sense of pride in seeing their work displayed. How are you building pride and ownership through student work samples?

Posters

Because my students were Black, I desperately wanted them to see images of Black people that went far beyond those in the media, pop culture stereotypes, athletes, and entertainers.

So, over the course of several years, I collected an abundance of historical and contemporary posters and pictures of Black individuals that ranged from civil rights icons to businesspeople and entrepreneurs and everything in between. I wanted the students to see images of people who looked like them who were either doing phenomenal work or whose work paved the way for them. How are you using posters and imagery in your classroom to build self-esteem?

Quotes

In an environment of intentionality regarding what students see, I wanted the walls to be an extension of who I was as their teacher and epitomize who we were as a culturally responsive learning environment where what the students saw mattered. To that end, I had quotes all over the classroom, and I used them to build my students' self-images. Although some of the quotes were those of famous people, the bulk were mine (because I wanted my students to be keenly aware that ordinary people like me had profound things to say). I would typically start the day or a new lesson with a quote that was connected to the direction of the lesson, and we would briefly discuss it. How are you using quotes in your classroom to build your students' self-images?

Classroom Name

Because I decided early on in my career that having my classroom identified by a room number was archaic, my students and I devised a name for the classroom—The Mind Zone, where, as the students said, "we take our minds and transform them into greatness." It *completely* changed the way that my students saw their classroom and made it stand out. Upon approaching the room, students were greeted each day by a big welcome sign beside the classroom door that read, "Welcome to the Mind Zone." Everything we did was preceded by the words *Mind Zone* (including our publishing company, Mind Zone Publications, where we published classroom essays as books). In what ways are you making your classroom stand out to build the self-esteem and self-images of your students?

The Teacher

Last, but not least, your students see *you*. When your students see you, what exactly do they see? Do they see a role model? Do they see an example of excellence? Do they see someone they can look up to? Do they see someone they can identify with? Do they see someone who genuinely cares about them? Do they see someone who plans for them thoroughly while being well organized? What message does your presence send to them? What message do your appearance and attire send to them? As their teacher, they see you, so you must be as intentional about yourself as you would about any aspect of your classroom.

I could write an entire book about the intentionality of what your students see. The intent here is to get you thinking about what your students see in your classroom and your objectives regarding what they see.

Q16 Toward creating a culturally responsive learning environment, how intentional am I about what my students hear?

In any given classroom, there is a percentage of children for whom it is not necessarily the norm to hear positive affirmations at home (which doesn't translate to the parents being careless or irresponsible; parents may not know, understand, or realize how powerful their words are). Words carry power and must be well thought out and used wisely. But if those same children never hear positive affirmations in their classrooms, they're likely going through life without hearing, for example, "You are somebody special," "You are extraordinary," "You are phenomenal," "You are amazing," "The sky is the limit," "The only thing that can stop you is you," or that their teacher will never give up on them and will always be in their corner. These words are powerful and impactful, particularly when they have intentionally become an inherent part of the culture of the classroom and when they are being expressed by someone who matters in the students' lives. When a youngster has the privilege of learning in a classroom that is overwhelmingly positive, the probability for his success increases exponentially. What are your students hearing from you? What are your Black students hearing from you? What impact do your words have on your Black students toward closing the achievement gap?

The intentionality of ensuring that your students are hearing positive words begins as soon as you see them in the morning with the way that you greet them. How you greet them coupled with your daily morning message lays a foundation and sets a tone for learning before instruction commences. What's key is the intentionality of what they hear from you at the start of the day and throughout the day toward creating a culturally responsive learning environment that remains positive.

Before moving on, let me leave you with this thought. Toward creating a positive learning environment where there is an intentionality about what students hear, be ever so mindful of the damage that you can do to a youngster through the use of deficit speech. For example, there was a time when I thought the term *at risk* was harmless and treated it solely as a designation. As I grew as a teacher and as a leader, it became crystal clear to me that *at risk* was deficit speech—whether it was used among colleagues about students or used directly with students. I eventually came to the conclusion that this language was unacceptable in either case. In other words, if a teacher sees a student as being at risk, that is the lens through which the teacher sees the student—and it's a deficit lens. I would rather the teacher see the student through a surplus lens as *at promise, at potential, at possible,* or *at probable.* That is a fundamentally different lens through which to view the student deemed at risk. Deficit speech is a reflection of deficit thinking, and when two or more deficit thinkers get together, a deficit culture is very likely to emerge. And it is the children who are inadvertently put at a deficit.

Q17 Toward creating a culturally responsive learning environment, how intentional am I about what my students feel?

The intentionality of what your students feel is absolutely critical. Here we are talking about students' emotions—what they feel in your classroom. This is an instance where your antennae must be all the way up because how students feel may not necessarily be visible. How do your students feel about themselves? How do they feel about who they are? How do they feel about how they look? Do they feel safe enough emotionally to be themselves? Do they feel free enough emotionally to express themselves? Are they emotionally safe from ridicule, harassment, and bullying from peers? Can they be themselves and resist the pressure to conform to the expectations of their peers? What does it feel like to be a student in your classroom, and what steps do you take to find out what they feel in your classroom? How does a Black student in your classroom, where the Black students are in the minority, feel in your classroom? Is this student emotionally safe in a classroom environment where there are so few Black students? Is your classroom a place where this student can feel emotionally secure? How do your Black students feel in your presence? Do you provide your Black students with a safe space emotionally? Are you welcoming to them? Is your demeanor pleasant? Is your tone pleasant? Are you approachable? Is building solid relationships and rapport with them a priority for you? How do they feel about you?

These are critically important questions to consider when creating a culturally responsive learning environment where there is intentionality about how your students feel. It is particularly challenging for children to learn in a classroom where they don't feel emotionally safe enough to be themselves.

> *Know this.* A student who hasn't been embraced by the in crowd and who tends to be a loner, doesn't dress like, speak the lingo of, or wear her hair in the style of the members of the crowd has the right to feel emotionally safe and secure, and it is up to *you* to lead the effort in creating an environment where this student—and all students—come to class every day feeling at home and emotionally safe.

Q18 Toward creating a culturally responsive learning environment, how intentional am I about what my students experience?

When your students have long since left your classroom and reflect on their experiences, what do you think they'll recall? Will they be able to recall having a magical experience, a memorable experience, or an experience rooted in high expectations? Will they be able to recall an experience that was inspiring or empowering? Will they be able to recall knowing that their teacher cared about them or something they looked forward to returning to every morning? Will they be able to recall a life-altering or life-changing experience? Will they be able to recall that they felt whole or that they mattered to you? Now reread these questions taking solely your Black students into account. Does this change any of your responses? Will they be able to conclude that their experience in your classroom contributed to who they are today? (When I reflect on my high school experience, I have zero positive recollections, not even about athletics. I feel nothing but anger.) These are important questions to consider as you reflect on your current practices toward creating and sustaining an intentional experience of cultural responsiveness for all of your students because you certainly don't want students to feel as I do when they recall their time in your classroom.

I can honestly say that I don't think a day goes by in my life where I don't ponder the thought of a former student showing up on one of my social media pages to inform me that his experience in my classroom was less than favorable. As long ago as my teaching days were, that would bother me immensely. My number one priority was creating a culturally responsive learning environment of excellence that made all students feel as though they mattered. I encourage you to make creating and sustaining a culturally responsive learning environment of excellence a top priority in your practice.

Q19 Do I bring the necessary cultural competence to my classroom toward engaging all of my students?

As a teacher of one or more content areas, you developed an expertise in the content area you teach and in teaching content to students. And because of your level of expertise both in your content area and pedagogically, I assume that you do the work that you do at a high level. What's key here is that you didn't develop your content area and pedagogical competence overnight. You developed it over time through a commitment to be competent. Cultural competence works the same say. When I say *cultural competence*, I mean getting to know your students through their lens as opposed to solely through your own. In other words, in a diverse classroom environment, it is a given that you will be surrounded by students whose cultures differ from your own, which provides great opportunities for everyone—including you—to learn from one another. This translates to an intentionality for not only being competent in your content area and pedagogically but also being competent culturally in connecting with racially diverse learners in your classroom and thereby meeting the academic, social, and emotional needs of all of your students.

Q20 What measures do I take toward increasing my cultural competence?

It all boils down to relationships and being intentional about getting to know your students—their unique experiences, realities, challenges, obstacles, needs, interests, goals, and aspirations. But you must also get to know them culturally. There are differences, and they can be significant. You've got to pay attention to them while suppressing and ultimately eradicating any cultural biases you may have. You've got to be intentional about getting to know your students culturally. We are not all the same, and we do not view the world in the same way. Our cultural experiences and backgrounds shape us, and, as the teacher, you've got to be mindful of this and demonstrate appreciation for it.

> *Know this.* As a principal, I have attended several funerals of either staff members or their loved ones who transitioned. The experience of the funeral of a white colleague was a dramatically different experience than the funeral of my Black colleagues. They were two culturally different experiences. I saw the movie *Black Panther* twice—first in a theater where most of the audience was Black, and again in a theater where most of the audience was white. They were two entirely different experiences culturally, relative to audience behavior. The white audience was very quiet, and the Black audience was very vocal (that is, many in the theater cheered, moaned, and clapped at the screen throughout, which is reminiscent of the call and response between the congregation and the pastor in a Black church).

Viewing the experiences through a cultural lens, I *completely* understood them both.

Classrooms are generally populated by students of diverse cultures, and their responses to various things will differ as greatly as do their cultures. If you, as the teacher, are culturally incompetent, incorrect conclusions will invariably be drawn about students because you're looking at the students through *your* lens as opposed to looking with understanding and clarity at students through their cultural lenses. When acquiring and sustaining cultural competence, you must learn your students as they learn content. You must be intentional about learning the overall experience of what it's like to be them and walk in their shoes. What does being your student mean? What would you experience were you to walk in their shoes? What are their realities? Do you understand the challenges that your immigrant students face as newcomers to a different country? Do you understand the challenges they may have faced when they left their home countries for America? There's *so much* to consider in developing cultural competence, but as a teacher of diverse learners, developing that competence is an absolute necessity.

CHAPTER 4

Equity and Culturally Relevant Pedagogy

Q21 What does it mean to be a culturally relevant practitioner?

As I noted in the Introduction, my foray into an independent study of African American history was life-changing. For the first time in my 23-year existence, I was learning about the history of my ancestors and about the Black experience in America beyond the limited view that I had up until then. It was a real awakening for me. I quickly discovered that I had been in the dark regarding who I was historically and that, unfortunately, I was not alone in that darkness.

The story of the Black man and the Black woman in America has historically been marginalized, distorted, or omitted from curricula in school districts throughout America. Black children aren't the only ones being denied the history of Black people. Children from all races have been denied the history of Black people, and many of them grow up to become teachers who were once denied as children, so it becomes a never-ending cycle of ignorance of the Black experience. Yes, there are always references to the period of enslavement in America (which, by the way, is the absolute worst period to which Black children should first be introduced; I'll elaborate in the next question), but they are typically superficial at best. And yes, important figures such as Harriet Tubman, Sojourner Truth, Frederick Douglass, Booker T. Washington, Mary McLeod Bethune, Rosa Parks, and Dr. Martin Luther King Jr. are often mentioned, but there are many, many more about whom students need to learn.

Learning all that I did about African American history gave me a tremendous amount of pride about being a young Black man. But maybe more importantly, what I read opened my eyes to my place in life. It told me that I had a role to play in the progress of the world. It told me that I could no longer stand on the sidelines or sit in the stands and watch others work. For the first time in my life, I was introduced to books in which there were people who looked like me beyond sports and entertainment and whose stories I could identify with along racial lines. Moreover, the world began to make sense to me because in learning African American history, I was learning about systemic racism and oppression in America and beyond that victimized Black people. I was learning about the historical relations between Black and white people in America, which was eye-opening and painful. I was experiencing an awakening to my societal challenges. It all started to make sense to me intellectually, and I wanted to do something about it. It soon became a no-brainer for me that my place was in the classroom teaching Black children. Two years after graduation, I started my education journey—and I've *never* looked back. African American history literally introduced me to myself.

What exactly happened to me? Learning for the first time was culturally relevant. I saw myself in the books that I read and, consequently, could identify with what I was reading. So, from day one as a teacher in that Brooklyn, New York, classroom, I was a culturally relevant practitioner:

> a teacher who utilizes a variety of instructional strategies that enable the students to continually see themselves culturally in their learning and who utilizes relatable learning strategies that the students can identify with through a cultural lens.

My objective for lessons, whether in math, science, language arts, or social studies, was to make learning culturally relevant for my students so that they could see themselves in what was being taught and identify with everything they were being exposed to. Regardless of the racial/ethnic composition of your classroom, to what extent can your students identify racially/ethnically with the lessons that you teach? Specifically, to what extent do your Black students identify with the lessons that you teach? I cannot overstate the significance of always considering who your students are racially and ensuring that they see the relevance in what they are being exposed to in ultimately closing all gaps in student achievement.

Q22 Who are my students, and will they be able to identify with or see themselves in my lessons?

As stated in the discussion on the equality mindset practitioner, you can never see your students as being the same. They are not. In fact, even if they are of the same racial/ethnic groups, they are still not the same. Each student is unique and is an individual. When devising your lesson plans, the question you should ask yourself is "Who are my students, and will they be able to identify with or see themselves in my lessons?" Can your Black students identify with what is being taught in your classroom?

After my fourth year as a certified teacher in New Jersey, I was named school, district, and county Teacher of the Year and was a finalist for New Jersey State Teacher of the Year. Many asked, considering that I hadn't taught for very long, what

I'd done to deserve such recognition and how my students were achieving at such high levels. I told them that I simply ensured that my students could identify culturally with what I taught. In other words, I put them in the lessons and on the pages. They saw the relevance of the lessons taught because I ensured that everything I taught spoke to them as Black students. I hadn't rewritten the curriculum; I breathed life into it and ensured that it wasn't generic. It was important to me that my students were able to connect culturally to *everything* that I taught.

Although I taught in predominantly Black schools, everything I've stated is applicable to racially diverse classrooms. In fact, there's something special about being culturally relevant in a diverse or even predominantly white classroom—it allows students to be exposed to and engage with multiple perspectives. Your white students and your students of color/non-Black students benefit immensely from being in such a learning environment because it enables them to see life through a lens other than their own. For example, in a history lesson on the Revolutionary War, textbooks historically painted a picture of all white soldiers fighting for the Continental Army and the British when, in actuality, between 5,000 and 9,000 Black soldiers fought for the Continental Army and more than 20,000 fought for the British after being promised emancipation from enslavement (which didn't materialize until years later). My point here is that the aforementioned information changes the entire paradigm and informs *all students* that Black men who were enslaved and promised their freedom fought for the colonies' independence from England and that the promises were broken and the enslaved were not freed until 87 years later.

I typically engage my audiences in an exercise when the discussion centers around culturally relevant teaching and learning. I hold up a sheet of paper and tell my audience that the paper is symbolic of a screenshot of the entire audience. I then ask my audience to, on the count of three, yell out who they would look for first in the photo—and, not surprisingly, everyone yells out, "Myself!" to which I respond, "Exactly." When I ask why they responded as they did, they reply that it's because, to them, they are the most relevant person in the photo. I then tell them that it works the same way in the classroom. Every day, children enter the classroom and, as they are walking in, the teacher symbolically hands them a class photo from the day before. When the students sit down and look at the photo, they notice that there are holes in the photo that represent the Black students. The Black students ask the teacher why they have been removed from the photo. The teacher, puzzled by the question, looks at the students, looks at the photo, and announces that she doesn't know how that happened and that she will attempt to fill the holes in the photo.

The student photo is symbolic of curriculum and instruction, where the absence of Black representation is obvious to the students. The Black students don't see themselves in the lessons or the pages of the books they're assigned. Their presence in the learning is invisible when, as in the example of the Revolutionary War, it should be *very* visible. In a culturally relevant classroom, regardless of the content area, Black children must be afforded the opportunity to see themselves toward ultimately closing the various gaps in achievement. When your Black students do not see themselves, it is very easy for them to quickly lose interest and disengage because the internal questions become "What's this got to do with me? How can I use it? How's it going to get me to where I one day want to be?" Therefore, the way that we approach curriculum and professional development must change radically. There is no equity in curriculum and professional development training that does not address the full representation of Black and Brown children. The absence of cultural relevance in professional development, curriculum, and instruction essentially boils down to children being victimized by a racist education.

Before closing out this question, I want to share a thought about teaching Black history. Hear me well: *The introduction of Black history can never begin with the period of enslavement!* Doing so can potentially make Black children mentally, psychologically, emotionally, and, in some cases, permanently deficient. It has the potential of simultaneously creating an inferiority complex for Black children and creating a superiority complex for white children. Instead, always start teaching students about Africa, where the disciplines of science, technology, engineering, mathematics, architecture, astronomy, agriculture, medicine, scholarship, writing, the arts, and so on are all a part of their ancestry. In other words, start them off with the high point of their history as opposed to the lowest point (when their ancestors were reduced to being considered chattel). This is necessary for both your Black students *and* your students of other races/ethnicities as it affects how your Black students see themselves and are seen by others. This matters exponentially, and your professional growth in this area is absolutely crucial.

Q23 Will my lessons allow my students to see the correlation between effort today and success tomorrow?

I want you to think about that student who was dealt an extremely difficult hand at birth. The youngster who was born into overwhelming strife and who faces challenges and obstacles rooted in poverty. That youngster in whose shoes a teacher who traded places for a day wouldn't last for five minutes. Well, that youngster is going to show up at school when he is 6 and may wind up in your classroom. My question to you is, will he be able to see the correlation between effort in your classroom today and success in his life in the future?

Imagine, if you will, that this youngster returns to a neighborhood every afternoon where the positive male role models are scarce and where crime, drugs, gangs, homicides—and hopelessness—abound. To what in your classroom will that youngster be excited to return every day? About what in your classroom will that youngster be inspired every day? About what in your classroom will that youngster feel empowered every day? With what lessons will that youngster be able to identify every day? What is it about you that will make that youngster look forward to being in your space every day? Will your lessons allow that youngster to see the correlation between effort today and success tomorrow?

I pose these serious questions for you to consider as an equitable practitioner operating within a culturally relevant learning environment. It's as important that your students see themselves in the learning as it is that they see the relevance in being in your class. While it's not unusual to conclude that undesirable student behaviors stem from challenges that need to be contended with, consider that the root of the behavior may be that the student sees the classroom as a place that has zero relevance to his life. Let that one marinate for a moment.

Q24 What measures do I take to ensure that I am growing as a culturally relevant practitioner?

Becoming a culturally relevant practitioner is a process. You can't just read a book, attend a training session, or watch a video and afterward declare that your approaches to teaching and learning are culturally relevant. There's much to learn and into which to fully immerse yourself. Becoming a culturally relevant practitioner starts by simply recognizing that there is, in fact, cultural diversity in your classroom. That can never be ignored in the name of equality. If there are two or more children of different cultures in a classroom, there is cultural diversity in that classroom. But then the questions for you become "What do I know about the cultures of the students in my classroom? What do I know about their cultures that ultimately informs who they are as children? What stereotypes or generalizations, if any, do I hold about the cultures of the children in my classroom?" Your answers to these questions are significant.

As an instructor—as a culturally relevant practitioner—your professional growth and development must be ongoing. This means that you must grow relative to learning who your students are beyond surface characteristics to the extent that you understand them culturally while putting yourself in a position to create lessons that speak to who your students are culturally. That will require that you be highly intentional about your professional growth in the area of culturally relevant teaching practices. There's a ton of information out there; you just have to avail yourself of it. (I have developed an extensive list of books for educators of Black children, divided up into categories, that you can access on my blog page at www.principalkafelewrites.com. It is an excellent resource for enhancing your professional knowledge of becoming a culturally relevant practitioner in your classroom.)

Q25 Did I have an intimate familiarity with people whose race is the same as that of my students/differs from mine prior to becoming a teacher?

This is something that I have discussed with white educators of Black children pretty regularly during lunch breaks of my workshops. When I work with a school with a large white teaching staff (typical in most parts of America) with a percentage of Black students, as we are having lunch time "edutalk," I request that someone speak about their intimate familiarity with Black *people* prior to becoming a teacher of Black *children*. I can recall one school where, during the lunch break, I was invited to sit with a group of teachers who were all white. After I made the request, the teachers instantly went from jovial and pleasant to tense and quiet, and they were visibly uncomfortable. (Now, before I go on, I want to say that I've met many white educators who have Black friends and I'm not implying that the reaction is universal.) As the group was now silent, I started to push: "Come on, now. I know that there's got to be *someone* at this table with a Black friend outside of work." As it turned out, none of the teachers had Black friends outside of work (which is understandable, given that many communities in America are racially homogeneous).

Since this was their reality, my natural follow-up was then "Does this mean that your initial intimate familiarity with Black *people* is pretty much through your Black *students?*" Silence once again. Although not the edutalk they anticipated, it was productive nevertheless. They all admitted that they only knew Black people through their students, pop culture, the media, sports, entertainment, passing each other at the store or the mall, and so on. I told them that they, therefore, had an abundance of work to do and that they could not fit their students into the equality mindset box because doing so would be detrimental to their academic, social, and emotional growth and development. I also told them that, as teachers, they had to fight with everything they had to prevent being influenced or driven by racist media stereotypes and generalizations about who and what Black people are.

I think the lessons those teachers learned during that lunch break were far more valuable than any in my six-hour presentation to their colleagues. This was that intimate, personal, uncomfortable conversation that I believe completely shifted their thinking about their priorities as teachers of Black children.

CHAPTER 5

Equity and Me

Q26 When I look at the faces of my Black students, my students of color, and other underserved students, who and what do I see?

I consider this to be a critically important question for any and all educators. I'm asking you what you see when you see your students. More specifically, what do you see when you look at the faces of your Black students, your students of color, and other underserved students? What do you see when you look into their eyes? Because, as their teacher, what you see is essentially who they are in your eyes. What you see in the faces of your students is reflective of what you believe they can accomplish as a result of being your students. If, for example, you see "at risk," then your students are going to be at risk. On the other hand, if you see "at promise" or extraordinary talent and ability, your students are going to rise to and meet your expectation. I can say this so definitively and with so much certainty because how you see them is going to dictate how you approach them and how you engage them. Why would your students need you as their teacher if you see them as incapable of achieving at high levels? If you see them as anything less than extraordinary, you are putting them at a deficit before uttering the first word of your first lesson. An equity mindset teacher is going to simultaneously see the greatness in all of students and realize that the vehicle to get them there will vary based on each student's needs. *That* is the epitome of equity.

Although we may all agree that the phrase "You must maintain high expectations" is cliché, it's unequivocally true. Your expectations *do* in fact matter, and they are life-altering for your students. I have placed a particular emphasis on the Black male learner because so many young Black males have been unjustly and unjustifiably written off by far too many in schools and beyond, and it is absolutely appalling and unacceptable. I was written off by many when I was young, but, thankfully, I had in my life enough of the right people—those who believed in my potential and possibilities—that I eventually went on to enjoy a successful career as an educator (despite having spent five years in high school and graduating with a 1.5 GPA). But it all boils down to what you see and what you believe when you look at the faces of your students. Do you see greatness, or do you see another negative statistic or stereotype? Your answer to this question matters exponentially.

Q27 How do I go about keeping the playing field level for *all* of my students?

I have obsessed over this question throughout my entire 33-year career. Before I walked into my first classroom in 1988, I learned that my assigned 5th grade class comprised a large number of students who had been left back once or twice. I was 28 at the time and knew with every fiber of my being that the students I was about to spend the year with had been the victims of an uneven playing field. I quickly learned that those students were extremely bright academically and that they knew the streets extremely well (given that most were older than average 5th graders). Between their grasp of the content that I engaged them in daily and what I learned of their lives outside school, I concluded early on that the sole reason that so many of my students had been left back was that they were essentially born into a world where their playing fields were unlevel. Certainly, poverty was an issue as *all* of them received free or reduced-price lunches—but I never allowed poverty to be *my* excuse. My intent was to receive my new students and begin the process of leveling the playing field via teaching practices that were rooted in forging culturally responsive relations with them while ensuring that the content that I taught was culturally relevant—that is, via equitable teaching practices.

How are you going about leveling the playing field for your students? How are you going about leveling the playing field for your Black students in particular, considering the ongoing gap in achievement between Black and white students? As I discussed in my ASCD book *Closing the Attitude Gap* (2013), I've always found the whole idea of an achievement gap problematic. The terminology alone implies that Black students have a deficiency. I am convinced that the achievement gap is a direct consequence of unlevel and uneven playing fields. Although as educators we possess neither the power nor the influence to level the playing field outside our classrooms, I firmly believe that we possess the power and influence to level the playing field within our classrooms, which translates into teachers having the power and influence to close the Black–white achievement gap in their classrooms.

Q28 Am I willing to embrace any possible implicit biases that I may possess but am unaware of that I may bring to my students?

It is a given that we all carry certain biases, in one form or another, that are not necessarily unhealthy or harmful. For example, I have a bias toward a particular make of car. I have a bias toward the color purple. And I have a bias toward particular genres of books, typically rooted in education and African American history. Those are not unhealthy or harmful things at all. They are essentially preferences. Biases become problematic when they are toward people and, in this case, relative to race, ethnicity, gender, culture, religion, class, sexual orientation, and so on. These are the biases that are harmful, hurtful, and divisive. They are dangerous and detrimental. They are particularly harmful when they show up in classrooms in the form of implicit or explicit biases. I will here focus on implicit biases in the classroom (as it is more than obvious that *explicit biases have no place in a school*).

When we talk about implicit biases, we are essentially talking about biases that are unconsciously possessed by a person. Although the person is unaware that he has them, because he does, they have a way of undermining the academic growth and development of his students and potentially compromising their opportunities toward maximizing their potential in the classroom. An example would be the paucity of Black youth in general in AP courses and Black males in particular. Hear me well: Black children are no less intelligent than any other children! Far more Black males than we currently see should be in AP courses. In this example, suppose the teachers of Black males at a given high school have bought into dangerous stereotypes about Black males and have concluded that an AP environment is inappropriate for Black males and keep them in lower-functioning learning environments (or refer them to special needs classes) because of implicit biases. It happens regularly. In this case, I'm referring to the implicit bias or soft bigotry of low expectations due to the internalization of false narratives about Black males.

With an equality mindset teacher, implicit biases are common because the students are being treated the same—equally—regardless of need. Such a teacher would be minimally inclined to come to grips with her implicit biases. An equity mindset teacher, on the other hand, is all in. That teacher is willing to embrace the notion that he may bring implicit biases to the classroom. This teacher wants to eradicate implicit biases because he views students as individuals with their own unique needs and wants to position himself to ensure that the needs of each student are being met (and, as a result, more Black male students may be selected for AP courses).

Who are you relative to implicit biases in your classroom? As you reflect on who you are in the classroom, is there any chance that implicit biases are manifesting in your interactions with and perceptions of any of your students? If so, are you willing to embrace them as areas that require immediate attention? Are you willing to accept that you may need to adjust your way of thinking? While evolving beyond biases is not easy, particularly if certain biases have been with us all of our lives, doing so is nonnegotiable as long as we bear the title "educator."

Q29 How do I ensure that disproportionality in handling student discipline doesn't exist in my classroom?

Throughout the equity portion of this book, I have frequently referenced the difference between the equality mindset teacher and the equity mindset teacher. I have known throughout my 33 years in education that the equality mindset just doesn't work. It has no place in a classroom because the consequences for students are dire in this environment. A case in point is the disproportionality of disciplinary referrals in schools. I have stated for years now that signs on classroom walls that read "Rules and Consequences" are problematic, and they are particularly pervasive in equality mindset classrooms. To eliminate disproportionality in handling student discipline, the language must change. The focus, rather than being on classroom rules (a micro approach), should be on classroom *expectations, norms,* and *values* and the overall culture of the classroom (a macro approach). Classroom rules are evidence of a one-size-fits-all mindset, which can be potentially damaging to students, particularly in a diverse learning environment. When rules are broken, for example, the social-emotional realities of students can never be ignored or dismissed because they, too, can factor into why and how the rule was broken. But if a given student is in a one-size-fits-all learning environment, there are going to be rules that all must adhere to equally, regardless of the individual needs and differences of the students.

Additionally, one must consider one's own disposition regarding how you see your students along racial lines. It has been well documented that there is large-scale disproportionality nationally in schools in the way that Black and white students are disciplined for exhibiting comparable behaviors. This is a reality that must be eradicated, and it begins with examining your discipline data, examining yourself, and ensuring that all students are being treated fairly and equitably.

Disproportionality in handling student discipline is very different in an equity mindset classroom; it won't occur. The individuality of each student will truly matter in this environment. As you bring an equity mindset to your classroom relative to meeting your students where they are academically, you must also be equitable with how you handle discipline. How do you ensure proportionality in handling discipline in your classroom? What do your discipline data reveal regarding which of your students receive the majority of the disciplinary referrals? What do your discipline data reveal regarding the racial breakdown of the disciplinary referrals? Are the behaviors in your classroom managed by expectations, norms, and values or by rules and consequences? The answers to these questions matter in the context of eliminating disproportionality in handling discipline.

Q30 Do all of my students have an equitable opportunity to learn and grow in my classroom?

With all that has been said in the previous questions, I will close out the equity section of this book with a culminating question: Do all of my students have an equitable opportunity to learn and grow in my classroom? This question really sums up everything I have written about in this part of the book. I challenge you to ask yourself this question daily—at the start of the school day before instruction begins, throughout the day as you engage in ongoing self-reflection and self-assessment, and at the end of the day as you reflect on the day. As I have written about extensively in other publications, self-reflection and self-assessment are powerful tools for self-adjustment and self-improvement. At the end of the day, all children deserve to learn in an equity mindset classroom led by an equity mindset teacher who engages students through equitable instructional practices that provide children with equitable opportunities to learn, grow, and develop.

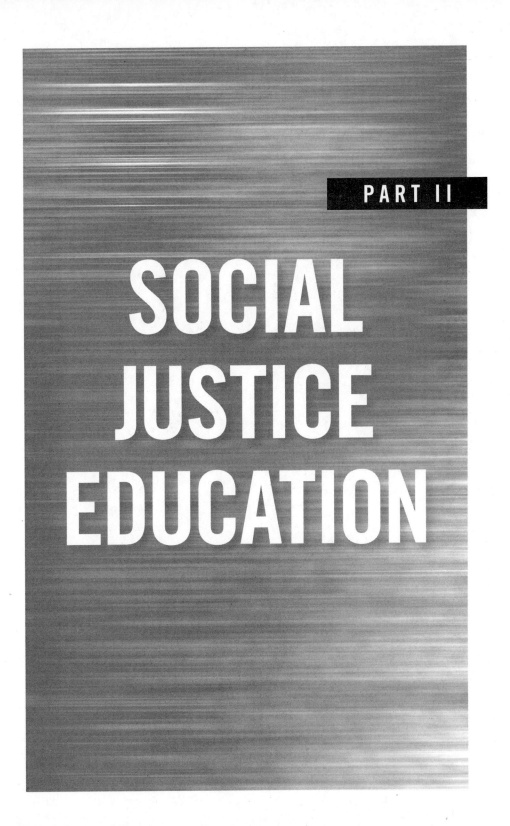

PART II

SOCIAL JUSTICE EDUCATION

CHAPTER 6

What Is Social Justice Education?

Q31 What do I know about social justice education?

As I stated in the Introduction, May 25, 2020, was a pivotal day in America. On that date, we were all introduced to George Floyd, and America shifted. Shortly thereafter, we were all introduced to Breonna Taylor. Interestingly, although the outcry following the killings of Mr. Floyd and Ms. Taylor was "Black Lives Matter," which became the focus of the summer of 2020, Black people weren't the only ones who were outraged, angry, fed up, and engaged in the fight for racial/ social justice and an end to police brutality and systemic racism. It was and continues to be a multiracial effort. Folks of all racial groups and countless nationalities from all walks of life gathered by the thousands across America and different parts of the world to proclaim that Black lives mattered.

As an educator, I watched everything unfold through an educator's lens, and I concluded that the deaths of Mr. Floyd and Ms. Taylor and the ensuing outrage would have school implications. In other words, I immediately thought about social justice education, including how and why we must get serious as a national educational community about incorporating social justice education into curriculum, instruction, and professional development, which is why I decided to make it a part of this book.

When I walked into my very first classroom as a teacher in 1988 in Brooklyn, New York, I walked into a classroom of 25 Black 5th graders as a social justice educator, not because I was trained to do so but because it just made sense. I didn't see the world and the classroom as two separate entities but rather as one and the same. It was clear to me that, as it related to issues of social justice, what happens in a classroom can impact the world and what happens in the world can impact the classroom. I saw a symbiotic relationship between the two and, hence, walked into the classroom as a social justice educator—and remained one throughout my two decades in public education.

To be clear, the current shift we are seeing across America is centered around social/racial justice for Black people. Although it's been a rallying cry for Black people for centuries, here we are in 2021, and there are so many from all walks of life, including educators, who have immersed themselves in the fight for social justice for Black people. My focus therefore will be social justice education relative to the Black community *through the lens of all of your students* toward simultaneously staying consistent with the times while responding to the demands of educators in general, and non-Black educators in particular, who have been reaching out to me relentlessly since the Floyd and Taylor killings for resources and strategies to incorporate social justice education into their curricula and instruction.

I felt that, as a starting point, I needed to define social justice education in a way that made clear what it is and what it is not. There are many solid definitions out there, and I have probably read most of them over the years. However, because I needed for this book a definition that was comprehensive, all-inclusive, and, most importantly, student-centered, I devised the following, which captures *all* of the elements of social justice education, and which will guide my writing for the remainder of the book:

Social justice education is the ongoing *student-centered* exploration, examination, and assessment of the world in which your students exist *through their own lens*. It's an *interdisciplinary* critical analysis of the world around them with respect to their relationship with it and how they fit in it via their own *self-expression* relative to issues of social justice, social injustice, and overall systemic, institutional, and individual racism, implicit or explicit.

Admittedly, it's a handful. I'll break it down in the next question.

Q32 What is my role as a social justice educator?

In the definition provided under the previous question, I high-lighted the following:

» Student-centered

» Through their own lens

» Interdisciplinary

» Self-expression

What these elements all have in common is that they are all about the student. The focus is on the student, not on the views and opinions of the teacher. While the teacher's role is vital, it's the views, opinions, and outlooks of the students that matter most. Let's look at each one separately.

Student-Centered

In the definition, I stated that social justice education is the ongoing *student-centered* exploration, examination, and assessment of the world in which your students exist. Here, I am talking specifically about your students' world, not *your* world. I am referring to an exploration, examination, and assessment of the way your students interact and engage with the world in which they exist—a large part of which typically includes the neighborhoods in which they live.

Through Their Own Lens

Here I am specifically addressing how your students see, envision, and interpret the world in which they exist from *their* vantage point—not from the vantage point of their teacher or one based on a generic explanation. How do *they* see the world as it exists for them *in real time?*

Interdisciplinary

Here I am stating that I am vehemently opposed to social justice education being treated solely as an add-on—that is, as an isolated discussion in a classroom, disconnected from everything else that happens in the classroom, inclusive of the content areas being learned. Instead, I am contending emphatically that social justice education has a place in a math lesson, science lesson, language arts lesson, social studies lesson, PE and health education lesson, and all other content areas that are offered in school, including career and technical education.

Self-Expression

What I'm saying here is that it is vital that students have a voice. This is yet another opportunity for students to be heard in their classrooms while simultaneously finding their own voice. Again, social justice education is not about the teacher's voice. While the teacher plays a significant role as facilitator, the views and opinions of the teacher should never be a central focus (as, if that were the case, we'd be talking about teacher-driven indoctrination and not social justice education).

Q33 What are the reasons that social justice education either exists or doesn't exist in my classroom?

Social justice education isn't new. It has been around for a long time but has sort of been confined to folks who consider themselves to be social justice educators. George Floyd's death brought the discussion of social justice education back to the surface. It's far from the forefront of the overall education conversation, however, but it is my hope that this book contributes to the broader discussion. As this question asks, what are the reasons that social justice education either exists or doesn't exist your classroom? Let's explore each reason separately.

Why Social Justice Education Exists in My Classroom

If a superintendent declares that there is a need for social justice education, the ball gets rolling as a result of the leader of the district. That is an ideal situation because it has the full support of the district leadership. At the building level, a progressive principal may decide that there's a need for the incorporation of social justice education in her school and, again, the rollout is backed by, in this case, the building leadership. And at the classroom level, there could be a scenario where, absent district-level or building-level mandates, you as a classroom teacher determined that there is a need to incorporate social justice education into your instruction (because, for example, it became obvious to you that there's a disconnect between social issues outside school and what occurs in the classroom, so you decided to bridge that gap and make social justice education a part of your classroom reality while remaining consistent with curricular mandates).

Why Social Justice Education Doesn't Exist in My Classroom

There may be countless reasons why social justice education doesn't exist in a school. One could be that it's neither a district-level nor a building-level mandate. To that, I will say to every superintendent or principal reading this book that *social justice education is essentially unavoidable if you truly want to connect the world to your classrooms.* They go hand in hand and enable students to make sense of it all when given the vehicle and platform to do so in a student-centered, interdisciplinary format.

Other reasons that social justice education may not exist in your classroom might include the following:

» You don't know where to start.

» You don't see the importance.

» You don't see the relevance.

» You feel there may be backlash from the parents.

» You feel there may be backlash from the community.

» You feel there may be backlash from your colleagues.

» You feel it may cause dissension in your classroom.

» You don't feel that you have the competence.

» You don't feel that the politics of the district/school will allow or support it.

I consider these valid reasons that may prevent teachers from proceeding with social justice education. One may conclude that they don't want to rock the boat and, instead, stay in their lane. I get it, but, in the long run, it's damaging for children. The key word here is *culture*. I would never ask a teacher to go out on a limb and risk employment (which is why I wrote this book for school and district leaders as well as for teachers). There must be an intentionality around establishing, building, and nurturing a culture around social justice education that extends to the community so that these most-needed conversations are palatable for *all*. While culture changes both attitudes and behaviors, there must be intentionality for a culture that is conducive to the sort of changes that are required for a true social justice education experience.

I deliberately left out one reason that social justice education may not exist in your classroom because I wanted to isolate it—*you don't feel that it is consistent with your political views*. All I really want to do here is remind you that nothing that occurs in a classroom is about us. It's about the children. Whatever our political views, whether or not they're consistent with what we should be doing for children, we need to check them at the building entrance before we walk into the school. Once we're inside the building, it's all about the children.

Q34 Can my students, particularly my Black students and my students of color, articulate, beyond emotional reactions, the injustices that surround them?

The motivation behind social justice education is to make students conversant in issues of social justice beyond emotional reactions. In a social justice education learning environment, students are able to go far beyond expressing emotions of anger, outrage, and disgust over issues that arise in the community (e.g., police shootings of unarmed Black men). In a social justice education environment, children can articulate a tragedy that occurred in a broader context. They can intellectualize it, understand its historical and contemporary implications, understand the data and statistics surrounding comparable situations, and draw intelligent conclusions. Moreover, as it relates to racism, they understand and can articulate the difference between individual racism and systemic racism.

It is particularly rewarding to listen to students express their thoughts about the injustices that surround them in a racially diverse classroom where non-Black students, who may not be directly impacted by a given situation along racial/ethnic lines, are able to express their views. What really stands out is how the non-Black students get to learn from their Black peers (who essentially become teachers) as well as from the teacher, and how they have the opportunity to hear perspectives from Black students, whom they may never have had an opportunity to hear or learn from, in a controlled environment. In the end, this is one of the goals of social justice education—to bring about understanding while increasing awareness across racial/ethnic lines.

CHAPTER 7

Social Justice Education and Classroom Instruction

In the first five questions in this chapter (35 through 39), I will provide examples for creating interdisciplinary social justice education lessons for math, language arts, science, social studies, and PE/health education, respectively, using as a theme the old Negro Leagues. (October 2020 marked the 100th anniversary of the first of several independent Negro League baseball organizations.)

For those of you who may be unfamiliar with the Negro Leagues, here's a brief history. Baseball, which originated in 1869 and is considered America's favorite pastime, became what we now know as Major League Baseball in 1903. From 1869 to 1947, Black players were not permitted to play alongside white players in the major leagues, regardless of the talent they possessed, solely because they were Black. Consequently, beginning in 1885, Black independent teams began to emerge, and they played each other until 1920, when the first of several all-Black leagues born of systemic racism—the Negro Leagues—was founded. (Bear in mind that barring Black players from playing alongside white players occurred prior to the landmark 1896 U.S. Supreme Court decision in *Plessy v. Ferguson*, which made racial segregation legal until the landmark 1954 *Brown v. the Board of Education* decision.) History has proven and recorded that some of the greatest baseball players who ever lived played solely in the Negro Leagues until 1947, when Jackie Robinson signed a contract to play for the Brooklyn Dodgers. As great as Robinson was, it is widely accepted that he was neither the best player to come out of the Negro Leagues nor the best player on his team, the Kansas City Monarchs (which speaks volumes about the caliber of the athletes who played in the Negro Leagues, considering that Robinson went on to become a Hall of Famer). After 1947, many Negro League players followed Robinson and signed with various Major League teams, dominated the game, and were eventually inducted into the Major League Baseball Hall of Fame.

The foregoing brief history of the Negro Leagues has both social justice implications and content-area implications.

Q35 How can I incorporate social justice into my math lesson planning?

While the history of Black people in baseball has endless social justice lessons, in terms of mathematics, there are countless lessons that can include how statistical indicators are calculated. Moreover, in a social justice context, the comparison of Negro League players' stats with the stats of Major Leaguers is quite revealing—and it is all mathematics. For example, while Babe Ruth eventually hit 714 home runs (a major feat) in Major League Baseball, over in the Negro Leagues, Josh Gibson was racking up 800 homers. There's a great deal of math intertwined with social justice in this comparison. Everything in life is numbers and, in the case of the Negro Leagues, the number of mathematical lessons with reference to social justice is infinite.

Q36 How can I incorporate social justice into my language arts lesson planning?

In a language arts classroom with a focus on social justice education, there are multiple activities in which a teacher can engage students in the areas of reading, writing, listening, speaking, and viewing. As I ponder the relationships between language arts, social justice, and the Negro Leagues, the possibilities are again infinite. The internet contains a wealth of information on the Negro Leagues—biographies of players and details of the many experiences that Black players had to endure in segregated America, which dictated where they could eat, sleep, use the restroom, shop, and so on. In addition to the internet, there's an abundance of researched information in the form of books and so much more that can be referenced when developing engaging lessons and discussions that heighten the conversations about issues of social justice relative to Black people throughout the course of American history.

In addition to the internet and books, YouTube contains a plethora of videos about the Negro Leagues that can be viewed. Lastly, when you incorporate writing, listening, and speaking, the possibilities for deep social justice learning activities with the Negro Leagues as a theme are endless.

Q37 How can I incorporate social justice into my social studies/history lesson planning?

History is probably the easiest content area in which to make the connection between content and social justice. Using the Negro Leagues as an interdisciplinary theme, there are numerous parallels. As the Negro Leagues were founded in 1920, World War I had recently ended (in 1918), which precipitated the beginning of the Great Migration of Black people to the Northeast, Midwest, and West. The Harlem Renaissance also began in 1920, and authors such as Zora Neale Hurston, Helene Johnson, Langston Hughes, Countee Cullen, and James Weldon Johnson wrote books addressing issues of racial injustice that are just as relevant today as they were 100 years ago. As much as times have changed, there is much that remains the same. Marcus Garvey's Universal Negro Improvement Association spawned the largest movement for social and economic change for Black people in recorded history and was at its height in this era. Racial injustice, racial oppression, segregation in all sectors of life, lynchings of Black men and women, race riots, and so on were the norm during this period and well beyond. And in the midst of all of this, the first of several Black baseball leagues was formed, with the Negro National League in Kansas City, Missouri, being the first.

Based simply on the information provided above, countless parallels can be made between American history, African American history (which is American history), and the reasons behind the formation of the Negro Leagues and the experiences of Negro League players that would aid in the incorporation of social justice education in lesson planning that bridges the gap between the classroom and the world beyond the school walls.

Q38 How can I incorporate social justice into my science lesson planning?

Let's say you're a secondary school science teacher of earth science, biology, chemistry, physics, or any of the other sciences, or an elementary school science teacher, and you're wondering how you can incorporate social justice education into a science lesson. Well, the possibilities are, again, infinite.

In keeping with the interdisciplinary Negro Leagues theme of this chapter, I want to zero in on physics. In a physics lesson, there is much that can be said about the velocity of a ball when it is released from a pitcher's hand, or the other position players' hands, after they catch a hit ball or after a ball is hit by a batter. Although very few records were maintained during the existence of the Negro Leagues, eyewitness accounts of many of the players (and of white players who played in exhibition games with Negro League players) indicate that some of those players were nothing short of incredible. One player in particular, Kansas City Monarchs pitcher Satchel Paige, was considered a legend because of his fastball. In a physics class, a discussion of the velocity of a baseball thrown by a pitcher can center around a discussion of Satchel Paige—a Hall of Famer who is considered one of the greatest pitchers of all time who, because he was Black, was not permitted into the Majors until 1948 (when he was 42, well past his prime and at an age when most players would have long since retired). The discussion could potentially be rich because, in Paige, we are talking about one of the best pitchers of all time who, were it not for the fact that he was Black, could have helped a Major League team win a championship during his prime. (The beauty, though, is that when Paige entered the Majors in July 1948 and joined the Cleveland Indians, he registered six wins against only one loss in helping Cleveland get to the World Series and win it as a 42-year-old pitcher! That speaks volumes about race in America.)

Q39 How can I incorporate social justice into my PE/health education lesson planning?

There are also infinite parallels between physical and health education and social justice education. Consider, during the age of COVID-19, the disproportionate numbers of Black men and women who contracted and died from the virus combined with the disproportionate numbers of Black men and women who do not have access to adequate health care or health insurance combined with the disproportionality of underlying health conditions such as diabetes from which Black men and women suffer. These are social justice issues because they're all rooted in systemic racism, and they definitely have a place in a health education classroom.

In terms of the theme of the Negro Leagues, it was difficult for Black baseball players to maintain a basic level of health, particularly in the South—where, because of legal segregation, the refusal of hotels, motels, and restaurants to admit Black ballplayers left them with no recourse but to do the best that they could regarding rest (players often went without sleep or slept in buses after playing as many as three nine inning games a day) and diet (they frequently missed meals).

In a lesson about maintaining good health through proper diet and rest, the experience of the Negro Leaguers is an excellent way to incorporate a discussion of social justice into the lesson (that is, how low wages, overwork, long bus rides, missed meals, and the denial of access to lodging due to race meant that the experience of being a Negro League baseball player took a heavy toll on the overall health of the athletes). The students would learn about maintaining good health in a lesson that parallels historical issues of social injustice, the necessary bridge to understanding the social justice issues of today.

With all that was said in this question and the preceding four, although I chose to focus on history as an interdisciplinary example, I cannot stress strongly enough that in order to fully grasp and understand the present, you have got to be armed with information about the past, because current realities do not operate in isolation; they are a part of an ongoing continuum (about which I will elaborate in the next chapter).

Q40 How could I go about planning interdisciplinary social justice lessons and activities in a self-contained classroom or with colleagues in a secondary learning environment?

At this juncture of your journey, what role does social justice education play in your lessons across content areas? What is your understanding of the social justice issues that impact your Black students? Do you see the potential parallels between the content area you teach and the social justice issues that impact your students? When developing lessons that adequately incorporate social justice education, you have to know your students far beyond who they are in your classroom, and you have to be familiar with the social justice issues that affect them. This would, in turn, put you in a better position to create lessons that are relevant to *all* of the students in your classroom, regardless of race and ethnicity. As an elementary teacher, you could accomplish this in collaboration with your elementary teacher colleagues. At the secondary school level, you could develop lessons with colleagues of other content areas, particularly at the middle school level, where students can be engaged in a group project with a social justice theme across content areas.

In the previous questions, I looked at social justice education through a historical lens using the Negro Leagues as my theme and outlined how it can be incorporated into interdisciplinary lessons across content areas. Contemporary social justice issues and instances abound and have a place in interdisciplinary instruction as well. Four issues that immediately come to mind are the mass incarceration of Black males (juveniles and adults), ongoing police killings of unarmed Black men, continued income disparities between Black and white families, and, in the age of COVID-19, the disproportionate number of Black deaths. All of these have interdisciplinary implications in classrooms.

CHAPTER 8

Social Justice Education and Professional Development

Q41 What type of professional development do I engage in to develop comfort and confidence in engaging my students in issues of social justice?

The reality is that we all come from different walks of life, and our experiences and realities are varied. As a result, in any given school, there's potential for a spectrum of staff members, ranging from those who are quite conversant in issues of social justice that relate to the students, to staff members who are grossly ill-informed, and everyone in between. Professional development geared toward understanding social justice issues that affect your Black students starts with learning the landscape of the community in which your students reside. Knowing your students at the classroom level is simply not enough. You've got to know them beyond who they are in your classroom. There's so much more to them than what you see of them in your classroom. They have experiences, realities, and challenges and face obstacles that are unique to African Americans and that are rooted in systemic racism. As a teacher, you must learn the communities in which your Black students live and the accompanying social justice issues—including, but not limited to, employment discrimination, housing discrimination, limited access to affordable health care, unsafe neighborhoods, inequities in education, voter suppression, and police brutality. Ways of doing this are through simple Google searches or reading online literature that speaks to the experience of a variety of Black students (e.g., Black students whose parents are from Africa or the West Indies/Caribbean as opposed to solely Black students born in the United students whose parents were born in the

United States). In addition, you must read books that journal the Black experience (some of which I'll list in the next question). You must also develop a level of comfort in engaging your Black colleagues and other Black people in your world who are willing to have the sometimes difficult, sensitive, uncomfortable but honest conversations with you in discussions about race and issues of social justice. The stories of the experiences of Black people you know or work with can be quite eye-opening.

(I can vividly recall on multiple occasions sharing my story with various audiences and seeing many wipe away tears. I often heard afterward, "I had no idea." They saw me as the person I am now and assume that my life was always comfortable. They didn't realize the racial barriers and obstacles I had to overcome to become who I am today.)

Rather than use this question to direct you to certain state and national professional development conferences and institutes, I'm instead strongly suggesting that you use what's right at your fingertips—online learning, books, and the human resources that are all around you.

Q42 What am I reading to further my understanding of social justice issues that directly impact my Black students and students of color?

Very soon after the death of George Floyd, I was literally inundated with e-mails and direct messages in my social media inboxes from educators who wanted information on and to understand what they were seeing on their televisions—marches, rallies, demonstrations, protests, rebellions, and rioting. They were also listening to countless interviews of Black people from all over the country—high-profile government, community, and business leaders; celebrities; and ordinary folks like you and me who had something to say about the then-current reality. To be clear, the inquiries were not coming from a racially diverse body of educators. They were coming exclusively from my white colleagues who teach Black children all over the country. Specifically, they wanted me to make book recommendations on, to use their language, "systemic racism, white privilege, and white supremacy." Many even told me that they desired a better understanding of their own privilege and how it adversely impacted Black people.

I knew exactly what books would meet their needs; I own many of them. But the teacher in me wouldn't allow me to recommend the books that I knew they wanted—that is, books that would deepen their understanding of systemic racism. My position was that once they read those books, there would remain a gaping hole in their understanding of racism because, although the books out there on contemporary racism are useful, relevant, and informative, I wanted these educators to have a *full* understanding of what got us to where we are today throughout history. In other words, I wanted them to be *conversant* in the history that got us here over 400-plus years. So I am suggesting to you the following four books that I suggested to every educator who reached out to me and which I recommend in equity and social justice workshops:

> » *Before the Mayflower* by Lerone Bennett Jr. I recommend this book because it will help readers gain a deep understanding of how we arrived at this place in

history, with a focus on the arrival of the first Africans to America in 1619 through the 1960s.

» *From Slavery to Freedom* by John Hope Franklin. This book focuses on the arrival of the first Africans to America in 1619 through the 1990s.

» *Introduction to African Civilizations* by John G. Jackson. I suggest this book because I want readers to have a sense of the history of Black people prior to the period of enslavement devoid of the racist depictions, distortions, marginalizations, and omissions we have been subjected to over the past four centuries.

» *The Mis-Education of the Negro* by Carter G. Woodson. Here's a book written in 1933 that could very well have been written in 2020. Every page in the book is as relevant today as it was in 1933 regarding the "miseducation" of Black students. Though not a history book (more of an analysis), it's one I fully recommend along with the aforementioned.

By no stretch of the imagination do I consider this list to be exhaustive. I have actually compiled a much more comprehensive list of books for educators of Black children that you can find on my blogsite at www.principalkafelewrites.com.

Q43 How knowledgeable am I on issues of social justice that directly impact my Black students and students of color?

In the previous two questions, I discussed your overall professional preparation for being a social justice educator and made suggestions for strengthening your understanding of social justice education in your classroom. Here, I am putting preparation aside and asking you the question in real time, "What do you know?" Depending on your familiarity with the issues surrounding the community of the students that you serve, this could in fact be an uncomfortable question—which isn't always a bad thing. Discomfort can be a motivator toward growth. In this regard, however, your knowledge of the social justice issues that directly impact your students is nonnegotiable. In education circles, we talk about relationships being at the core of everything that we do. I am in full agreement with that. But when your students are in your classroom, they are not there in a silo, isolated from the world outside. When they walk into your classroom, they bring the world outside along with them because they are a product of it. You are a product of your world, I am a product of my world, and *your students are products of their world*—a fact that you can never ignore.

What do you know about the social issues in the communities in which your students reside? What do you know about the impact that these issues have on your students? What do you know about the world in which your students exist? Issues of social injustice in areas such as employment, housing, living conditions, safety, health care, education, and police brutality are indeed real in the Black community. And as they impact Black residents in your school's surrounding neighborhoods, they impact the children who are enrolled in your school and on your classroom roster. If you are going to know your students fully in general and your Black students specifically in this regard, it is incumbent on you to gain a full understanding of the social issues they contend with and the social injustices that they grapple with on a daily basis. Although these issues may or may not be a part of your reality, they could very much be an inherent part of your students' reality, which, in turn, makes them an inherent part of your professional reality as an educator of Black children in a world where systemic racism continues to be a national reality.

CHAPTER 9

Social Justice Education and My Reality

Q44 Can I relate to the issues of social justice that directly impact my Black students and students of color?

Depending on your reality, you may consider this yet another uncomfortable question. As one who pays attention to national and world affairs, I hear the varying viewpoints on a variety of sociopolitical issues. The world is diverse, and we see it through our own unique lenses. However, when one makes the decision to teach, and to do so in a community that is very different from the one in which she lives or grew up in, it becomes incumbent on the teacher to learn about and get to know both the students and their neighborhoods.

When I taught and led in the city of East Orange, New Jersey, I knew that city inside and out—every street and the social issues—because I was born and raised there. In contrast, when I launched my career in Brooklyn, New York, although I had a vague understanding of the borough, and some of the challenges were similar to those in New Jersey, I didn't have an intimate knowledge of it. If I was going to fully know, understand, and appreciate the world in which my students lived, I needed to acquire detailed knowledge of the section of Brooklyn in which I worked and to learn about the issues that affected my students and their families.

As I learned about the issues, because I am Black, as were my students, I was able to fully relate to the issues their families grappled with. Can you relate to the issues that directly impact your students of color? Can you relate to the issues that directly impact your Black students? Do the issues that directly impact your Black students make sense to you? Do your political views allow you to see your students through the lenses through which they view themselves? Do your political views prevent you from relating to and identifying with the realities of your students (which may differ greatly from yours)? These are critical questions that you must come to grips with as an educator. Regardless of what we believe, our politics, or our values, once we step foot into that classroom, it's all about the students we serve and relating to them through their lenses.

Q45 Do the issues of social justice that directly impact my Black students and students of color impact me personally?

In other words, are the social justice issues that your students' families grapple with the same as those you might grapple with?

As I write, I am taken back to a day in the early '90s when I suffered a humiliating experience while driving home from school after having taught all day. I was wearing a navy blue suit, a white dress shirt, and a yellow tie (I'm old school and dressed that way when I was a teacher), and, as I drove past a local park where many of my students hung out, I was followed by and pulled over by the police. The officers rudely told me to step out of the car and spread my legs and spread my arms and hands on top of the car. They searched me for a gun. When I asked them why I'd been pulled over and searched, they said I fit the description of an armed suspect they were looking for (and eventually informed me that I was not who they were looking for). In the park adjacent to where this was happening were throngs of students from my school—including some from my class. I had to do damage control when word got out to the administration and colleagues that "Mr. Kafele was searched by the police."

In neighborhoods like that one across America, such occurrences are commonplace. Nearly everyone knows someone who experienced something similar or experienced it themselves. What I endured is normal for countless residents in Black neighborhoods all over America. What about you as a teacher of students of color and Black students? Have the issues of social justice that directly impact your students of color impacted you personally? When you see injustices occur in your students' neighborhoods, can you identify with them on a personal level? When you see injustices occur in your students' neighborhoods, can you empathize with the reactions of community members? Do you advocate on students' behalves? As relationships are an inherent component of student success in the classroom, you must do all that you can to get to know your students and their families beyond their classroom environment toward fully relating to who they are, their experiences, and their realities as Black residents in their community.

Q46 Am I perceived by my students as someone credible enough to engage them in discussions of social justice?

If, for example, a teacher who teaches math continually struggles with the content, the students will figure out in no time that they have a teacher who lacks competence in teaching math, and the teacher's credibility as a math teacher will be undermined. I can vividly recall my year as a substitute teacher, filling in for different science teachers. I didn't know science then (I don't know it now), and the students knew it and didn't take me seriously as a substitute science teacher. (They knew my area of expertise was in African American history and encouraged me to teach it to them.) Well, it works essentially the same way regarding engaging your students in discussions of social justice. Credibility matters.

You are not in a position to incorporate social justice into your content area or to engage your students in discussions of social justice if you do not know and understand the issues that they, their families, and their communities face or if your worldview or politics are diametrically opposed to your students' realities. This is why I stated that you must learn the world of your students and become relatable to your students. They know their reality. They are living their reality. They feel the pain of their reality. They know their truth. You can't come in and change their truth because you see the world differently or live in an environment that differs dramatically from the one your students live in. Your role is to aid in making them successful, and their success journey will be born out of their realities—whatever they may be. *Issues of social injustice that are impediments to success can never be ignored.* They are your students' truths. So the question becomes, based on what you know of the social justice issues that your students, their families, and their communities are confronted by, do your students perceive you as someone credible enough to engage them in discussions about these issues? Do your students perceive you as someone who's interested in these issues? Do your students perceive you as someone who cares about these issues? Do your students perceive you as someone who can help them to overcome or deal with these issues? Your credibility as a social justice educator matters as a teacher of children in general and as a teacher of Black children in particular. Therefore, it's incumbent on you to focus on becoming a great teacher of children as well as a great teacher of content.

Q47 Do my colleagues and I dialogue to understand issues of social justice and collaborate regarding incorporating social justice education into our lessons?

As I stated elsewhere in this book, the emphasis that I have placed on the Black child relative to equity and social justice is because this book was conceived in the aftermath of the killings of George Floyd and Breonna Taylor. If the two of them were alive today, I wouldn't have written this book at this juncture in my life. As an educator, I knew instinctively that their deaths and the national outcry "Black Lives Matter" would have school implications. It *must* have school implications. The reality is that not every educator in every school across the country is prepared or equipped to dive into incorporating social justice education into lesson planning—it requires a great deal of research, studying, learning, and collaborating with colleagues.

It is my strong opinion that collaboration around issues of social justice cannot be circumvented. While professional development is vital, it must culminate with internal discussions among staff. The biggest challenge is when a school comprises staff who just don't know the issues that their Black students are facing or when the staff is so detached from the lives of students beyond the school walls that they are oblivious to their students' realities. Staff coming together is vital toward having a book study (on a book such as this one) when working to incorporate social justice education into your lessons. What makes the process a little easier is when you have colleagues who are knowledgeable about the issues and who are in position to help staff make sense of the world of their students. To what extent do you and your colleagues discuss issues of social injustice that impact your students' lives? To what extent do you and your colleagues collaborate on incorporating social justice education into your lessons? To what extent do issues of social justice matter to you and your colleagues? As with anything else in education, discussion and collaboration on these important issues are imperative.

CHAPTER 10

Social Justice Education and Racial Justice Education: Are They the Same?

Q48 How do I distinguish social justice education from racial justice education?

While social justice education and racial justice education are equally important, they are not synonymous. The difference between the two? Race.

Toward being politically correct and minimizing discomfort, unease, and tension, framing the injustices of the Black community with the language of social justice education can minimize the possibility that the work environment will become volatile during discussions. But if we are talking about injustices that groups face relative to the color of their skin, then at some point we have to be courageous enough to transition into the conversation of racial justice education because the members of the groups are being victimized, mistreated, oppressed, and so on solely because they belong to a particular racial group. Yes, racial justice education falls under the umbrella of social justice education, but it is your responsibility to become knowledgeable enough and comfortable enough to be able to talk to your students using the language of racial justice, regardless of the racial group you belong to. How comfortable are you with having conversations about racial justice with your colleagues and students? If you are not a Black educator, are you comfortable engaging colleagues and staff in conversations about racial justice issues? Is the infusion of racial justice education one of your school's priorities?

Ideally, you won't be operating in a silo because everyone in your school will be on the same page and committed to infusing racial justice into the curriculum and instruction.

Q49 Am I open and willing to engage my colleagues in the tough, critical, and sensitive but necessary conversations about race, systemic racism, and racial justice?

I can attest to the fact that conversations about race, racism, and racial justice can be quite intense, particularly with a racially diverse staff. Those conversations, however, are *necessary*. If we fail to have these conversations, we are doing children a grave disservice. My motto: If it impacts the students, we must be willing to discuss it.

The year 2020 was interesting on so many levels. I can honestly say that it has been decades since I witnessed and experienced racial tension to the degree that I did then. (Although I was born in 1960, I was too young to understand what that decade really meant in real time.) Issues of race are not and cannot be separate and apart from school, particularly if there are Black students in your school. If your school has Black students on the roster, then I can tell you definitively that race is an issue in your school, whether you recognize it or not, and it will be manifested via your various data streams. Again, to understand race, systemic racism, and issues of racial justice, you've got to develop an understanding and appreciation for how we got where we are over the past 400-plus years. You've got to study history. In the summer of 2020, in the context of the racial landscape, America learned of two critical moments in history regarding African Americans that the Black community has been familiar with for decades: the 1921 one-sided race riot (more accurately described as a massacre) that resulted in the burning down of Black Wall Street, in Tulsa, Oklahoma, a self-contained, economically robust community populated by African Americans; and Juneteenth (short for June 19, 1865), when the enslaved population of Texas was finally informed of their emancipation—two months after the end of the Civil War. Many non-Black people across America only learned about those events following the Floyd and Taylor killings because they were not included in history books. Those incidents and countless similar incidents are why we are where we are today, but far too many of us—and far too many of us in the education community—are unaware and underinformed.

I share all of this to say that, as a teacher of Black children, you must be open, willing, and courageous enough to engage your colleagues in the tough, critical, and sensitive but necessary conversations about race, systemic racism, and racial justice. However, it is imperative that your knowledge base and that of your colleagues runs deep. Because the pain of Black suffering is, as I frequently say, *ancestral-deep*, you won't fully understand it if you haven't developed an understanding of African American history. Are you and your staff having these critical conversations? Are you comfortable having these critical conversations? Are you comfortable initiating these conversations when others are not? A major component of equity and social justice education is having the courage and the audacity to be an advocate with an activist spirit for the students you serve.

Q50 Do I have the self-efficacy to engage my students in the tough, critical, and sensitive conversations about race, systemic racism, and racial justice?

Of all of the self-reflective questions in this book, I think that this one is the most personal. This is the question that really compels you to reflect on how you responded to the previous 49 questions. It's the beginning of the path to self-discovery. It essentially requires that you ask yourself, "Who am I when I am in my classroom with my Black students?" It is asking you about your confidence in yourself about engaging your students in difficult conversations about these sensitive topics. In short, it's asking you who you are when you step into the classroom.

I don't have much to say on this final question; it's all about you. Now that you've read this book, who will you be when you next walk into the classroom? Leaders, who will you be when you walk into your school?

Do you have the confidence, the belief in yourself, and the courage to make learning real and relevant for your students? That is the question.

Conclusion

I read the original manuscript of this book over several times before sending it to the publisher for editing. The subject of this work is, admittedly, a departure from that about which I've written over the years—school leadership—and focuses on topics about which I'd only, until now, presented. However, in light of the deaths of George Floyd and Breonna Taylor, I was strongly compelled to put my thoughts on equity and social justice education in the book that you now have in your hands.

Any and all aspects of social and racial justice have historical implications. In order to fully understand contemporary social and racial justice issues, as I indicated previously in the book, you have to understand what got us to this point. You have to understand history relative to Black–white relations. As an educator of Black children, what do you know about the history of Black people in America? How familiar are you with the past four centuries of Black existence in America? As I close, I brainstormed 50 self-reflective questions for you to ponder ranging in topic from the arrival of the first Black people to America all the way to "Black excellence," which continued to manifest throughout the past four centuries despite having to endure some of the most heinous oppression known to humans. By no means is this an exhaustive list of questions. In fact, it started as 3 simple questions, then 5, then 10, then 20, then 25, then 35, and I decided to cap it at 50. As a teacher of Black children specifically but a teacher of children in general and regardless of the subject areas that you teach, I challenge you to look at these questions in earnest and to take a deep dive into those that you might struggle with. Your students deserve a well-informed teacher as each of the themes of these questions impacts your Black students in one way or another.

1. What do I know about the circumstances upon which the first Africans arrived to America?

2. What year and location did the first Africans arrive?

3. What do I know about the Middle Passage?

4. What do I know about Black participation in the Revolutionary War?

5. What do I know about the intricacies of the "peculiar institution" known as enslavement?

6. What do I know about the abolitionist movement, including the rise of the Black press?

7. What do I know about the *Dred Scott* decision?

8. What do I know about the Emancipation Proclamation, including Black participation in the Civil War?

9. What do I know about Juneteenth?

10. What do I know about the Black Codes?

11. What do I know about the 13th Amendment?

12. What do I know about the 14th Amendment?

13. What do I know about the 15th Amendment?

14. What do I know about the reason for HBCUs?

15. What do I know about the reason for Freedmen's Schools?

16. What do I know about the reason for the Freedmen's Bureau?

17. What do I know about the intricacies of Reconstruction?

18. What do I know about the Compromise of 1877?

19. What do I know about *Plessy v. Ferguson?*

20. What do I know about the founding of the NAACP?

21. What do I know about the Garvey Movement?

22. What do I know about the Harlem Renaissance?

23. What do I know about the Negro Leagues?

24. What do I know about the plethora of inventions and discoveries of Black inventors and scientists?

25. What do I know about the history of lynchings of Black men and Black women?

26. What do I know about the history of race riots and white mob violence toward Black men and women?

27. What do I know about Black Wall Street?

28. What do I know about the Rosewood Massacre?

29. What do I know about the Tuskegee Experiment?

30. What do I know about the Great Migration?

31. What do I know about Black participation in World Wars I and II and the Tuskegee Airmen?

32. What do I know about *Brown v. the Board of Education?*

33. What do I know about Emmett Till?

34. What do I know about the Montgomery Bus Boycott?

35. What do I know about the Little Rock Nine?

36. What do I know about the Greensboro Four?

37. What do I know about the 4 Little Girls?

38. What do I know about the March on Washington?

39. What do I know about Bloody Sunday?

40. What do I know about the treatment of Black soldiers after the Vietnam War?

41. What do I know about the civil rights movement?

42. What do I know about the Civil Rights Act of 1964?

43. What do I know about the Voting Rights Act of 1965?

44. What do I know about the Black Power Movement?

45. What do I know about COINTELPRO?

46. What do I know about the Black studies movement?

47. What do I know about the struggle for Black racial justice beyond the '60s and '70s?

48. What do I know about the historical and contemporary tensions between the Black community and the police, which include the mass incarceration of Black men?

49. What do I know about contemporary issues of racial and social justice in the Black community?

50. What do I know about the infinite number of examples of "Black excellence" that has existed since the arrival of the first Africans to America as indentured servants and subsequently throughout the period of enslavement through the present?

Had I been asked any of these questions before I was 23, my answer would simply have been "Nothing." As I became a voracious reader of African American history at 23, I became fixated on this information. I was obsessed, and it became my world and gave me an immeasurable advantage as a teacher and, subsequently, leader of Black children. Delve into the books that I mentioned in this book—*Before the Mayflower* by Lerone Bennett Jr. and *From Slavery to Freedom* by John Hope Franklin—to gain invaluable insights into the fullness of African American history.

It is my hope that this book will significantly impact how teaching is approached in classrooms across the United States, and abroad, and particularly in classrooms in which at least one Black student is present. Equity and social justice can *never* be add-ons to the current repertoire. Instead, they must be natural, organic, and inherent parts of what you do every day. And when they are, you'll be doing your part to change the world!

Acknowledgments

I want to thank Mrs. Joy Scott Ressler, my editor, for bringing to this book the magic that she brought to both *The Assistant Principal 50* and *The Aspiring Principal 50;* ASCD content acquisitions director Ms. Genny Ostertag, for continually believing in me; and Stefani Roth, for always, always having my back. I remain grateful for the three of you.

Bibliography

Bennett, L. (1982). *Before the Mayflower: A history of Black America.* Chicago: Johnson Publishing Company.

Delpit, L. (2006). *Other people's children: Cultural conflict in the classroom.* New York: The New Press.

Franklin, J. H. (2000). *From slavery to freedom: A history of African Americans.* New York: McGraw-Hill.

Gay, G. (2000). *Culturally responsive teaching: Theory, research, and practice.* New York: Teachers College Press.

Hale, J. E. (1982). *Black children: Their roots, culture, and learning styles.* Baltimore: Brigham Young University Press.

Jackson, J. G. (1970). *Introduction to African civilizations.* Secaucus, NJ: Citadel Press.

Kafele, B. K. (2009). *Motivating Black males to achieve in school and in life.* Alexandria, VA: ASCD.

Kafele, B. (2013). *Closing the attitude gap: How to fire up your students to strive for success.* Alexandria, VA: ASCD.

Kafele, B. K. (2016). *The teacher 50: Critical questions for inspiring classroom excellence.* Alexandria, VA: ASCD.

Kafele, B. K. (2019). *Is my school a better school because I lead it?* Alexandria, VA: ASCD.

Kafele, B. K. (2020). *The assistant principal 50: Critical questions for meaningful leadership and professional growth.* Alexandria, VA: ASCD.

Kendi, I. X. (2019). *How to be an antiracist.* New York: Random House.

Ladson-Billings, G. (2009). *The dreamkeepers: Successful teachers of African American children* (2nd ed.). San Francisco: Jossey-Bass.

Lomax, L. (1968). *To kill a Black man.* Los Angeles: Holloway House Publishing.

Love, B. (2019). *We want to do more than survive: Abolitionist teaching and the pursuit of educational freedom.* Boston: Beacon Press.

Riser-Kositsky, M. (2020, June 16). Education statistics: Facts about American schools. *Education Week.* Retrieved from https://www.edweek.org/leadership/education-statistics-facts-about-american-schools/2019/01

Tatum, B. D. (1997). *"Why are all the Black kids sitting together in the cafeteria?" And other conversations about race.* New York: Basic Books.

Woodson, C. G. (1933). *The mis-education of the Negro.* Washington, DC: Associated Publishers.

Index

About the
Author

 **B**aruti K. Kafele, a highly regarded urban educator in New Jersey for more than 20 years, has distinguished himself as a master teacher and a transformational school leader. As an elementary school teacher in East Orange, New Jersey, he was named East Orange School District and Essex County Public Schools Teacher of the Year, and he was a finalist for New Jersey State Teacher of the Year. As a middle and high school principal, he led the transformation of four different New Jersey urban schools, including Newark Tech, which went from a low-performing school in need of improvement to national recognition, and which was recognized by *U.S. News & World Report* as one of America's best high schools.

Kafele is one of the most sought-after school leadership experts in North America. He is the author of 12 books, including ASCD book *The Aspiring Principal 50* and his six ASCD best sellers—*The Assistant Principal 50*, *Is My School a Better School Because I Lead It?*, *The Teacher 50*, *The Principal 50*, *Closing the Attitude Gap*, and *Motivating Black Males to Achieve in School and in Life*. He is the recipient of more than 150 educational, professional, and community awards, including the prestigious Milken National Educator Award and the National Alliance of Black School Educators Hall of Fame Award. He was inducted into the East Orange, New Jersey, Hall of Fame, and the city of Dickinson, Texas, proclaimed February 8, 1998, Baruti Kafele Day. Kafele can be reached via his website, www.principalkafele.com.

Related ASCD Resources

At the time of publication, the following resources were available (ASCD stock numbers in parentheses).

Print Products

The Aspiring Principal 50: Critical Questions for New and Future School Leaders by Baruti K. Kafele (#120023)

The Assistant Principal 50: Critical Questions for Meaningful Leadership and Professional Growth by Baruti K. Kafele (#121018)

Becoming the Educator They Need: Strategies, Mindsets, and Beliefs for Supporting Male Black and Latino Students by Robert Jackson (#119010)

Closing the Attitude Gap: How to Fire Up Your Students to Strive for Success by Baruti Kafele (#114006)

Cultural Competence Now: 56 Exercises to Help Educators Understand and Challenge Bias, Racism, and Privilege by Vernita Mayfield (#118043)

Even on Your Worst Day, You Can Be a Student's Best Hope by Manny Scott (#117077)

Five Practices for Equity-Focused School Leadership by Sharon I. Radd, Gretchen Givens Generett, Mark Anthony Gooden, and George Theoharis (#120008)

The Innocent Classroom: Dismantling Racial Bias to Support Students of Color by Alexs Pate (#120025)

Is My School a Better School Because I Lead It? by Baruti K. Kafele (#120013)

Keeping It Real and Relevant: Building Authentic Relationships in Your Diverse Classroom by Ignacio Lopez (#117049)

Motivating Black Males to Achieve in School and in Life by Baruti K. Kafele (#109013)

The Principal 50: Critical Leadership Questions for Inspiring Schoolwide Excellence by Baruti K. Kafele (#115050)

The Teacher 50: Critical Questions for Inspiring Classroom Excellence by Baruti K. Kafele (#117009)

Digital Products

DVD: *Motivating Black Males to Achieve in School and in Life* with Baruti K. Kafele (#611087)

For up-to-date information about ASCD resources, go to www.ascd.org. You can search the complete archives of *Educational Leadership* at www.ascd.org/el.

ASCD myTeachSource®

Download resources from a professional learning platform with hundreds of research-based best practices and tools for your classroom at http://myteachsource.ascd.org/

For more information, send an e-mail to member@ascd.org; call 1-800-933-2723 or 703-578-9600; send a fax to 703-575-5400; or write to Information Services, ASCD, 1703 N. Beauregard St., Alexandria, VA 22311-1714 USA.

WHOLE CHILD
TENETS

1 **HEALTHY**
Each student enters school healthy and learns about and practices a healthy lifestyle.

2 **SAFE**
Each student learns in an environment that is physically and emotionally safe for students and adults.

3 **ENGAGED**
Each student is actively engaged in learning and is connected to the school and broader community.

4 **SUPPORTED**
Each student has access to personalized learning and is supported by qualified, caring adults.

5 **CHALLENGED**
Each student is challenged academically and prepared for success in college or further study and for employment and participation in a global environment.

THE**WHOLE**
CHILD

The ASCD Whole Child approach is an effort to transition from a focus on narrowly defined academic achievement to one that promotes the long-term development and success of all children. Through this approach, ASCD supports educators, families, community members, and policymakers as they move from a vision about educating the whole child to sustainable, collaborative actions.

The Equity & Social Justice Education 50 relates to the **safe** *and* **supported** *tenets.*

For more about the ASCD Whole Child approach,
visit **www.ascd.org/wholechild.**